DATE DUE

NO 18 '99			
DE 8 '99			

DEMCO 38-296

Competing
Realities

COMPETING REALITIES

The Contested Terrain
of Mental Health Advocacy

SUSAN MEYERS CHANDLER

PRAEGER

New York
Westport, Connecticut
London

Library of Congress Cataloging-in-Publication Data

Chandler, Susan Meyers.
    Competing realities : the contested terrain of mental health
advocacy / Susan Meyers Chandler.
        p. cm.
    Includes bibliographical references.
    ISBN: 0-275-93356-3 (alk. paper)
    1. Mental health services—United States.   2. Mental health
    policy—United States.   I. Title.
    RA790.6.C398   1990
    362.2'0973—dc20   89–22815

Library of Congress Catalog Card Number: 89–22815
ISBN: 0-275-93356-3

First published in 1990

Praeger Publishers, One Madison Avenue, New York, NY 10010
A division of Greenwood Press, Inc.

Printed in the United States of America

∞

The paper used in this book complies with the Permanent Paper Standard issued
by the National Information Standards Organization (Z39.48-1984).

10 9 8 7 6 5 4 3 2 1

This book is dedicated to all persons coping with mental illnesses.

Contents

Acknowledgments

While I was working on this book, I was frequently asked, "Why are you interested in writing about people with mental illnesses?" People asked me why I continue to go to state legislatures again and again to make the point that mental health services are inadequate, that funding is insufficient and planning nonexistent. People frequently ask me if I have a "sick person" in my family, as if that would explain my interest and commitment.

In reality, my concern for people with mental illnesses comes from the knowledge that this problem can strike anywhere, to anyone, at any time. And this is coupled with the fact that wherever it occurs, help is usually poorly provided and effective services are few and far between. Most people just don't seem to care about this social problem or the millions of people it afflicts. That is why I have written this book.

This book is based on my work over the last five years with the Mental Health Association in Hawaii. However, my earliest interest in the field of mental illness was shaped by Drs. Thomas Scheff, Steve Segal, and Troy Duster at the University of California. Later, I was continuously prodded and inspired by the intelligence, analytical skill, dedication, and compassion of Dr. Sheila Forman at the Mental Health Association in Hawaii.

I wrote a significant portion of the book while at the National Center for Social Policy and Practice, National Association of Social Workers. Dr. Karen Orloff-Kaplan provided a supportive environment (along with an office and a computer) that sped the book along to completion.

My colleagues at the School of Social Work at the University of Hawaii helped in a variety of ways. Ms. Hisae Tachi, in particular, is one of those people who always knows where things are and easily and graciously lends a helping hand.

I would like to thank my parents, Helen and Saul Meyers (who both actually proofread the book!). Their clear vision for a better society and commitment to all disadvantaged people has been a beacon for my professional work. To my husband, David, whose good cooking and superb parenting skills kept the family together while I wrote and rewrote—I appreciate your participation in this accomplishment. And to my son, Michael, I hope that this book may shed a little light on a huge social problem, so that you and your generation will live in a more accepting and more humane world.

The Persistent Problems of People with Mental Illnesses

The problems of people who are seriously and persistently mentally ill are vast and complex. While there is general awareness about the scope and severity of this issue, its extent is still unknown. Documenting exactly how many people suffer from mental illnesses is difficult for several reasons. First, there is still a stigma attached to having a mental illness, which results in a reluctance to admit or report it; thus there is a significant underreporting of the true prevalence. Second, the complex array of existing treatment systems—from the public, state hospitals to the exclusive, private clinics with fee for service practitioners—makes finding, monitoring, and following up on mentally ill people difficult. Third, the variety of diseases labeled mental illness and the varying prognoses among individuals diagnosed with the same illness make estimating its frequency and prevalence difficult.

ESTIMATES

The published estimates of the number of people suffering from a mental disorder at any given point in time is about 10 percent of the total population (Brown, *The Transfer of Care*, 1985). Using a frequency count in the community, the Midtown Manhattan Study found that 23 percent of the adult population in New York City were affected by a serious psychiatric impairment at any point in time (Srole et al., 1962).

More recent studies estimate that 15 percent of the population is affected by a mental disorder in a one-year period (Current Population Reports, Bureau of Census, 1987). As newer techniques of case identification are developed, the numbers increase. Public health epidemiologists now estimate annual prevalence rates of more than 20 percent of the population per year will suffer some form of mental illness. That is, approximately 48 million American adults suffer from a mental-emotional disorder at some time during their lives (Torrey,

1988). More than 9.5 million children under the age of 18 also suffer from mental-emotional stress. The annual cost of mental illnesses to society is more than $54 billion in reduced productivity, lost employment, direct clinical care, and social welfare programs. It is estimated that more than 50 percent of patients seeking medical help do so because of physical symptoms related primarily to stress reactions or emotional problems. Depression-related suicides take more than 20,000 lives each year; another 85,000 die from alcohol-related causes; drug abuse kills and maims thousands more.

Of all illnesses requiring hospitalization, mental and emotional disorders are at the top of the list. They represent 30 percent of the total number of hospitalizations—more than cancer, heart, and respiratory diseases combined. Mental illness accounts for 12 percent of total estimated health care costs but receives only 4 percent of health related research funds. By contrast, cancer accounts for 8 percent of health care costs yet garners more than 29 percent of the federal research dollar. Only $4 per capita is spent on research related to mental disabilities in the United States against $150 per capita on cancer and heart research (Torrey, 1988).

THE DEVELOPMENT OF A SOCIAL PROBLEM

Mental and emotional disorders consume a staggering proportion of the country's human and financial resources. Yet mental illness has not yet become a widely discussed social problem. Spector and Kitsuse (1973) suggest that there is a natural history, development, and selection process that brings social problems to the forefront of American concerns. For example, unemployment, while always a problem to those actually unemployed, did not become a "true" social problem with acute public awareness and national concern until more than a third of the entire population were unemployed during the Great Depression. Then, the federal government initiated the New Deal to come to grips with the problem of unemployment.

As yet, the public does not seem to "see" mental illness as a serious social problem. Fear of stigmatization keeps family members from seeking treatment for an ill relative; mentally and emotionally distressed persons themselves often fear the label of mental illness and the discrimination it entails. The responsibility for the majority of mental health treatments and service delivery has become dispersed among private psychiatrists and other allied health care professionals. There is little public responsibility or mandated accountability at the state or federal level to care for mentally ill persons. The mentally ill themselves and/or their families attempt to find a route through the maze of mental health services searching for the elusive appropriate help.

Major Mental Disorders

In most cases, mental illnesses are amenable to treatment, and effective intervention results in restored mental health. However, for the seriously and persistently mentally disabled, this is often not the case. Estimates of the numbers of persons suffering from major mental disorders (e.g., schizophrenia and major depressive disorders) range from two to three million people in the United States (Torrey, 1983). If family members are included, the problems associated with these mental illnesses affect more than 15 million people.

In the United States, one out of a hundred people will be afflicted with schizophrenia, with more than 600,000 people being under treatment each day. One hundred thousand people are diagnosed as having schizophrenia for the first time each year. The cost of treating and maintaining these people, who are often both psychologically and financially unable to care for themselves, has been rising steadily. Now, more people are hospitalized for mental illness than for heart disease, cancer, diabetes, and arthritis combined. The cost of caring for the schizophrenic illnesses alone totals more than $30 billion in state hospital costs, medical treatment, disability payments and welfare. Another $10 billion vanishes in lost wages. Major mental disorders are the most expensive of any of the chronic diseases. These costs do not include those mentally ill persons with less serious diagnoses and those who never receive treatment or the benefits due to them. Nor do they include the tremendous and costly burdens that family members pay, both financially and psychologically. While there has been much discussion about the deinstitutionalization of the mentally ill into communities (or onto the streets as part of the homeless population), more than 65 percent of schizophrenic patients discharged from hospitals return to their homes and families.

The Costs

By the end of the twentieth century, the cost of mental illnesses will be as high as $142 billion a year, including $24 billion in direct expenditures for treatment programs, research and training programs, and building and construction. Indirect costs of $29 billion come from lost employment, reduced productivity, absenteeism, and premature death due to mental-emotional disorders. Ten to twenty percent of the

American labor force are considered "troubled employees." They have been identified as having stress disorders or having problems with alcohol and drug abuse. Few of these workers ever participate in mental health programs, receive counseling, or attend employee assistance programs in spite of their proven effectiveness. Most do not seek help because of the stigma associated with being mentally handicapped. Ironically, the 1987 Kenneth Donaldson Award of San Antonio's Mental Health Association, given annually to a former mental patient who has made an outstanding contribution to the community, was not picked up that year. The reason was that the winner was afraid that his boss would learn of his past illness, threatening his current employment status!

The Stigma Remains

Historically, the mentally ill have been ostracized, abused, ignored, and segregated—expected to make it on their own. Today, while there is much more knowledge and information about the etiology, progression, and effective treatment regimens, there is still a lot of fear and misinformation on mental illness as well as vigorous debate among mental health professionals about what is known and what solutions exist.

Schizophrenia is the most controversial of the mental illnesses. Even finding agreement among mental health experts as to what exactly comprises a schizophrenic illness is hard to accomplish. Some think that schizophrenia is more than one disease entity. Doctors frequently disagree over the initial diagnosis. Then there is a variety of opinion as to what actually causes schizophrenia. Theories range from genetic predisposition, biochemical imbalances, nutritional abnormalities, and family system dysfunctions, to an infectious virus that remains dormant in the brain for many years before fully developing into florid symptomatology. There is an unfortunate degree of agreement among the ranks of those who discriminate against mentally ill persons. They believe that mentally ill people are unpredictable, violent, will decrease their property values if they live in their neighborhood, can never be cured, and are best treated in hospital settings far away from populated areas.

The Problems Remain

Thus, while controversy continues to surround the etiology, treatment, and care of mentally ill persons, their obvious needs, which include housing, medical care, income support, personal support, and psychiatric care, are well defined. There has been significant improvement in some aspects of their care and treatment. Yet thousands of people still do not benefit from these improvements; tragically, the young people who are just becoming afflicted with mental illnesses foresee a bleak future in terms of appropriate services and programs. In place of the mental institutions that at times functioned as an isolated asylum that both segregated and protected mentally handicapped persons, the system of mental health services today is accurately described as a fragmented array of programs, often uncoordinated and inappropriate, epitomized by the decaying state hospital. The newest "facility of choice" for many young, newly diagnosed mentally ill persons is the streets. The streets offer nothing to the chronically mentally ill person but the freedom to live as he or she "chooses," primarily because the other choices (i.e., mental health programs and services) are either too restrictive, too costly, not available, or nonexistent.

Many books have been written about the needed reforms in the public mental health system (Morrissey, 1985; Tessler and Goldman, 1982; Brown, 1985; Talbott, 1984; Stein and Test, 1985). Critiques of the mental health commitment laws are also plentiful (Ennis and Emery, 1978; Scheff, 1966). The entire community-based system of care is currently under attack as an approach that was politically unfeasible and woefully underfunded. Strident complaints have been heard from the consumers themselves and from their families. More recently, the professionals are being blamed for the failure to bring about an improved mental health system. Even our institutions and social structure have been named as the primary culprit.

NEW STRATEGIC APPROACHES

Strategies believed to improve the treatment and care of the seriously mentally ill have ranged from micro level analyses to macro level interventions. At the micro level, recent study and attention have focused (again) on biological causes of mental illnesses. The "new biologism" is a reflection of the biochemical directions of researchers in the field and the heavy influence of psychoactive medications as the major form of treatment, particularly with psychoses. Family systems and interpersonal psychotherapies are now being reserved for the "worried well" whose mental health problems are more easily handled with brief therapeutic interventions. At the other end of the spectrum for reform are the organizational and systemic schemes that prescribe new forms of planning models stressing improved coordination among mental health agencies and organizations, better service delivery systems, and more focused responsibility between the private and public care sectors.

With so many strategic approaches and so much new research, with a broad knowledge base and enhanced professional expertise dedicated to solving the problems of the mentally ill, why are the solutions so elusive? If we know so much about the problems of the mentally ill, why are we unable to effectively assist the millions who suffer? With the combined efforts of patients, their families, professionals from social work, psychology, psychiatry, and nursing, advocates and community activists, why are the problems so seemingly intractable?

THE PLAN OF THE BOOK

This book attempts to explain this phenomenon by looking at the problems of mentally ill people and the system of care designed to help them from several different perspectives. The major themes discussed include the differing definitions of mental illness and its etiology, and the differing treatment technologies that have logically developed from the differing definitions of the problem. Preferred interventions continue to be variable, resulting in confusion and continuous debate. There are varying theories as to the structure and design of the system of service delivery that effectively organizes the array of services appropriately and efficiently. And there are policy dilemmas that lead to inconsistent and inequitable treatment. Are these problems impossible to solve? This book will structure a framework around which many of the conflicts delineated may be resolved. The purpose of this book is not to add to the many other criticisms of the existing mental health system, nor repeat the litany of past failures. Rather, it documents and demonstrates that there are wide areas of agreement among the disputing professionals, advocacy groups, family members, and the consumers themselves. There are broad zones of agreement among the disparate groups that could bring the separate pieces of this tragic puzzle together. The book offers to those interested in mental health reform practical strategies to bring about the needed changes.

Patterns of failing social policies for seriously mentally ill persons are reviewed. The author looked for the "zones of agreement"—the consensus areas where professionals and advocates agree on the problem definition and the manner of solution. Rather than pleading for a better society that will accept the seriously mentally ill, or suggesting that a new and coordinated system is just around the corner if only there were more money, this book examines the *conceptual* problems in this field; the *professionals' dissonance* about the definition of the problem and the strategies for success; *the patients' and family members'* views of their needs, and *the competition among advocacy groups—all attempting to "help."* This book offers practical suggestions for improved policy and programmatic approaches based on a *conflict resolution model of change.*

The organization of the book is as follows:

Chapter 2 analyzes the recurring themes and issues that have surrounded the field of mental health since its earliest conception. Historical, economic, political, and sociological views are described. Special attention is given to the implications of the policies of deinstitutionalizing hospitalized mentally ill persons. Legislative initiatives since World War II are examined with a focus on their impact on patient care and the development of a community-based mental health system.

Chapter 3 examines the failure of the deinstitutionalization policies for the seriously and persistently mentally ill. This chapter reviews the *intended outcomes* of the recent legislation, policies, and demonstration programs designed to provide high quality, comprehensive mental health services. Then the chapter describes the *unintended consequences*—such as (1) the rising readmissions into state hospitals of previously released patients; (2) the phenomenon of "trans-institutionalization"—the rise of new for-profit industries such as nursing homes, single room occupancy facilities, boarding and care "homes," and welfare hotels for the mentally disabled; (3) the increasing visibility of the homeless; and (4) the rising number of young adults who are being labeled as "chronically" mentally disabled but who have never been hospitalized because admission criteria to state hospitals have been tightened.

Chapter 4 examines the changing roles and responsibilities of the state governments, the local governments, families, mental health providers, and welfare agencies. An apparent "transfer of care" was to take place, with much of the mental health system abdicating its responsibility for the mentally ill. The policy shift assumed that as the mental health system surrendered its control of its mentally ill clients, the welfare system would accept them and provide the necessary care. This task on top of an overextended state welfare system has proven to be overwhelming. A second shift of care was to take place. A shift to "privatize" and contract publicly mandated services to private-sector providers has not brought about the intended improvements expected with increased competition for patients. Issues regarding inherent interdisciplinary competition, as well as areas ripe for collaboration, are examined. The new interorganizational arrangements and new public/private mechanisms of service delivery are described.

Chapter 5 looks at models of advocacy. What is this term that is so commonly understood, yet so poorly defined? Models of advocacy are described as well as the government influence on its ebb and flow in relation to mentally ill persons.

Chapter 6 reviews thirty years of politics from a mental health advocate's point of view. The commitments and promises of the 1960s, which were made by government, were moved into private hands more and more in the 1980s. The practical nature of this shift is discussed and analysed.

Chapter 7 describes the prominent advocacy organizations that essentially define the field of mental health, and looks at the frameworks and belief structures that pervade the different perspectives of these groups. This chapter examines the perspective of mental health professionals and attorneys and lays the foundation for understanding the reasons behind their differences and similarities.

Chapter 8 discusses the "advocacy wars" among the organizations and agencies whose goal it is to help the mentally ill. It looks at the needs and positions of consumers, family members, and other advocates. Each group has goals, objectives, strategies, and perspectives that attempt to assist the mentally ill. This review outlines the tensions that exist among advocacy groups advocating for improved services for mentally ill people. Several examples are used to delineate the differences between service-oriented advocates and civil rights advocates. Organizations such as the National Mental Health Association, the National Alliance for the Mentally Ill, and the National Mental Health Consumers' Association all have the goal of improving services for mentally ill people, but their strategies and approaches vary significantly and their disagreements may in fact be hurting the group they are intending to help. Citing and describing their differences is easy. This chapter begins to explore the areas of overlap upon which consensus can be built.

Chapter 9 begins to delineate a negotiation strategy for meeting the needs of mentally ill people. The chapter focuses on the rise of the National Alliance for the Mentally Ill (NAMI). This newest of the advocacy groups for the mentally ill has grown rapidly, and as a self-help group for the family members (usually parents of seriously mentally ill adults) has become a new force on the mental health scene. Their insistence on biochemical causes as the sole etiological factor for the onset of schizophrenia has brought them into conflict with several of the traditional mental health professionals, other advocate groups, and primary consumers. They have been most critical of mental health professionals, who often see the problems of the mentally ill in "family" or "systems" terms. The chapter describes their national agenda and strategies for altering the definitions of mental illness, and for reeducating professional mental health workers who disagree with their points of view. The chapter discusses the parallel growth and development of patient rights groups and of the "family rights" groups, which often have different perspectives on what is necessary to improve the lot of the mentally ill. Patient rights versus professional judgment versus parent views is a newly forming triad that needs to be understood and is explored in this chapter.

Chapter 10 reviews two particularly difficult types of conflict common in the field of mental health. This chapter examines in depth the conflict between the rights of returning patients to live on their own in a community and the concerns of the community to "protect" the mentally ill as well as their environment. The famous case of Joyce Brown, a homeless woman living on the streets of New York City, is detailed to highlight this type of dispute.

Chapter 11 outlines the knowledge that is necessary to understand the complex issues surrounding the mentally ill and the skills necessary to work successfully in this field. This chapter focuses on mezzo levels of intervention. Case material demonstrates how to form successful coalitions for legislative action and manage problem solving groups for solutions. This "how-to" chapter follows a grounded theoretical framework and problem definition. It should be particularly useful for mental health workers and advocates, but may also be of use to mental health consumers and their family members.

2

Recurring Themes: Progress and Retreat

The circumstances of most of the seriously and persistently mentally ill are much better today than one hundred years ago. Over 146 years ago, Dorothea Dix began her crusade to convince the Massachusetts State Legislature that family members of the mentally ill alone could not, and the local community would not, be able to care for insane persons. Conditions for any mentally handicapped person who could not live with their family or alone in the community were abominable. The mentally ill, even those incapable of knowing the difference between right and wrong, were languishing in jails along with paupers, criminals, retarded citizens, and other persons whom the community then deemed were best off in secure, punitive, custodial environments. In most cases, these "residences" were a mixture of the English workhouses and the United States' effort to build facilities for one class of society that the dominant classes rejected. Dix argued that small, geographically isolated *treatment* hospitals should be designed to help and protect the mentally handicapped. Many were convinced that such a program of treatment would actually cure the insane and that after a short stay, many would be returned to the community as productive citizens. Buoyed by the successes of Dr. Philippe Pinel's "moral treatment" approach in France that stressed a nurturing, caring, supportive program of treatment for the mentally ill, a "cult of curability" emerged in America (Deutsch, 1937). However, shortly after the first state hospitals were built, they became overcrowded and the demand greatly exceeded the availability of beds. Parallel with the increased demand came increased methods for controlling the patients and a subsequent decrease in the rate of success. In only a few years, the optimism that social reform could improve the lives of the seriously mentally ill was sharply waning. Hospitals were rapidly replacing the other facilities that housed these social rejects, but attempts at moral treatment yielded to very little treatment of any kind. Care retreated into control, physical restraints, and seclusion (Gruenberg and Archer, 1979). Now the mentally ill were out of the sight of the communities, and although not receiving adequate treatment or assistance, their pleas were silenced due to their physical isolation and their social stigma.

INSTITUTIONAL REFORMS

In 1908, with the publication of Clifford Beers' book, *A Mind That Found Itself,* attention refocused on the mentally ill. Clifford Beers, who had lived for several years in a psychiatric hospital, wrote eloquently about the poor living environments and at times brutal treatment of the mentally handicapped living in state institutions. His efforts led to the founding of the National Association of Mental Hygiene (NAMH) in 1909. The original focus of this group was to improve the care and treatment of mental hospital patients. The association was concerned with needed social reform and saw the need for housing the poor as inextricably linked to the problems within the hospitals. The group understood the connection between securing housing and the release of hospitalized patients. This "foresight" was rediscovered in the 1980s by the National Institute of Mental Health with its community support system approach to the chronically mentally ill.

Unfortunately, the reform efforts of the NAMH were set aside as the country entered World War I. Psychiatrists turned their attention to preventing psychiatric disorders primarily through early detection and psychotherapeutic interventions. Tremendous support went to devising theories of child guidance and a renewed emphasis was put on parent education to prevent mental illness. While these efforts were admirable in that the problems of childhood mental illnesses were being identified for the first time, they had little effect on the persons with chronic and seriously disabling mental disorders who were already living in hospitals, nor would they be effective in arresting the development of later psychoses.

FREUD'S PROFOUND INFLUENCE

The influence of Sigmund Freud during the 1920s and 1930s has left a lasting mark on the mental health treatment methodologies and service delivery system in the United States. It is almost impossible to overestimate Freud's influence in any discussion of the development of community-based psychiatry. Freud's approach of having a patient "struggle with his disorder," rather than the doctor diagnosing, treating, and curing the patient, altered the doctor-patient relationship dramatically (Gruenberg and Archer, 1979:489). Doctors began to independently sell their time, talent, skills, and attention to patients *outside* of (and apart from) psychiatric hospitals. Psychiatrists also could now be selective in which patients they chose to treat; if psychotherapy was not effective, it was just as likely to be considered the patient's "fault" for not working hard enough as it was the doctor's lack of skill or an inappropriate intervention. Gruenberg and Archer (1979) contend that the commercialization of the provision of psychiatric services laid the foundation for psychiatric careers to emerge unconnected to state hospital facilities.

THE IMPACT OF WORLD WAR II

World War II also had a profound influence on the system of care of the mentally ill. Several events occurred almost simultaneously to push a somewhat apathetic nation into action towards increasing the support for mental health services. First, the nation was shocked to learn that twelve out of every hundred men examined for military induction were rejected for neuropsychiatric reasons. Of all those rejected by the draft for any reason, 39 percent had a neuropsychiatric diagnosis (Levine, 1981). Considering that the men rejected were only that sample of physically healthy men between the ages of 18–37, serious concerns about the magnitude of the mental health problem in America emerged. Second, many conscientious objectors who were required to work in public facilities as alternative service to fighting the war began working in state psychiatric hospitals. These men, many of whom were politically active, well educated, and influential, began to report and publicize the deplorable conditions they saw in these hospitals. And third, psychiatrists were becoming quite successful with crisis intervention techniques that were very effective in treating soldiers suffering from the stress and trauma of their war experience. The psychiatrists were publicizing the success of new treatment techniques that were brief and on an outpatient basis.

THE NATIONAL INSTITUTE OF MENTAL HEALTH

The federal government responded to these new circumstances by passing the National Mental Health Act of 1946. It created the National Institute of Mental Health (NIMH). NIMH received federal funds to provide research and training grants, grants-in-aid to those states wishing to develop community-based psychiatric services. The enabling legislation required that each state design or designate a mental health authority to receive the funds and establish a planning, fund disbursing, and governing mechanism. No funds were to be spent on patient care in state hospitals. The goal was to develop a system of outpatient care that would eventually decrease the need for state hospital beds. This optimistic approach in retrospect seems foolhardy, since the dilapidated, understaffed state hospitals would be receiving no additional federal funds and the states had been notorious in their neglect. Thus, while the number of mentally ill persons being admitted to the state hospitals continued to rise, new impetus was shifting the focus of care away from the state institutions. The designers of the NIMH legislation believed that by developing a system of community-based, mental health outpatient services, earlier diagnoses would occur that would prevent some hospitalizations and save the states money. They also believed that hospitalized patients could now be released earlier and treated on an outpatient basis, further decreasing costs. These dreams of cost cutting to the states, however, were never realized. Hospital costs kept increasing concurrent with the community care systems' growth and costs.

An unintended consequence of the new infusion of federal funds into mental health services was the rapid increase in the number of university-trained mental health professionals and the expanded opportunities for private practice outside of the state institutions. The state hospitals could not attract or maintain highly trained psychiatrists, who now saw the private sector developing into a more lucrative and innovative alternative for their practice.

TREATMENT INNOVATIONS

Again in the early 1950s, several events occurred simultaneously to dramatically change the circumstances for the seriously mentally ill in the United States. Gruenberg and Archer (1979) contend that the major impetus for the deinstitutionalization of state hospital patients was a series of reports by three British mental health directors, Duncan MacMillan, T. P. Rees, and G. Bell, who not only substantially changed the atmosphere of their psychiatric hospitals, but changed the entire treatment orientation towards the seriously mentally ill. These administrators opened up the locked wards, removed restraints from the patients, and halted involuntary hospitalization. The changes resulted in long-term stays in the hospital being replaced with longer-term stays in the community. Efforts were made to insure that a single treatment team, made up of a psychiatrist, nurse, and social worker, was maintained for each patient. This team followed the patient from the hospital into the community and vice versa. Hospital episodes of care were made readily available in times of crisis, but the thrust of the care was now to achieve successful living in the community.

The reports of the successes with this approach were at first received with skepticism in the United States. It was not until the World Health Organization granted a fellowship to study the programs that American hospital administrators began to reexamine their own patterns of treatment and care inside state hospitals.

Drug Innovations

The debate still rages among mental health policy experts and researchers as to the exact role that psychoactive and/or neuroleptic drugs played in the huge shift of patient care from inpatient to outpatient localities. Some note that the decrease in the number of patients living in hospitals occurred before the massive use of the antipsychotic medications and that deinstitutionalization policies, financial cuts, and milieu therapeutic approaches were responsible for the shift of patients out of the state psychiatric hospitals. But most agree that the antipsychotic medications made the deinstitutionalization of mentally ill persons much easier and quickened its pace significantly. In 1953, the drug chlorpromazine was administered to seriously psychotic patients with remarkable results. Doctors began to report that the drug was able to bring about a calming affect on seriously disturbed patients. Many believe that without the widespread use of antipsychotic medications, many of the seriously mentally ill patients would never exhibit enough "appropriate" behavior to permit them to leave the "protection" of the hospital. When taking such drugs, most seriously mentally ill persons are tranquilized so much that most of their "bizarre" behavior disappears. By 1955, these drugs were being used extensively throughout American psychiatric hospitals as the treatment of choice for psychotic patients. However, as has been frequently noted, these drugs have severe and unpleasant side effects. They are almost universally disliked by the patients who are told by most psychiatrists that they must take them in order to live successfully outside of the institutions.

THE START OF DEINSTITUTIONALIZATION

In 1955, the state hospitals were still the major location for the treatment of psychiatric episodes (Brown, 1985). However, for the first time, the 1955 statistics reported a decrease in the number of persons residing in hospitals (Talbott, 1978). The *loci* of care had started to shift from the vast, centralized state institutions to smaller, more varied, community-based programs. The resident population in state hospitals was decreasing from a high in 1955 of 558,000 to approximately 140,000 in 1979, a reduction of almost 75 percent (Taube and Barrett, 1983).

By 1971, state hospitals accounted for only 19 percent of psychiatric episodes, with 20 percent already being accounted for by community mental health centers. That figure grew to 29 percent by 1975. By 1979, the hospital proportion had fallen to only 9 percent of the total episodes of inpatient and outpatient care (Brown, 1985). Outpatient care had increased dramatically from 379,000 clinical episodes in 1955 to 4,600,000 in 1975, a twelve-fold increase in twenty years (Kiesler, 1982). Kiesler makes the crucial point that while everyone was looking at the huge decrease in the number of episodes in state and county mental hospitals, from 819,000 in 1955 to 599,000 in 1975, these numbers were obscuring the fact that the number of total hospital episodes was actually increasing by more than 38 percent between 1955 and 1975 (Vischi et al., 1980). Thus, while state hospitals were being deinstitutionalized, psychiatric units of general hospitals and VA hospitals, along with private psychiatric hospitals, were *increasing* their patient load by almost equal numbers. While NIMH supported a policy of deinstitutionalization and the development of outpatient care, the funding mechanisms inherent in the Medicare and Medicaid programs had strong fiscal incentives that favored hospitalizations (as do most insurance reimbursements schemes). As policy makers at NIMH spoke glibly of deinstitutionalization and watched the numbers of residents in state hospitals disappear, clinicians and for-profit hospital administrators followed the reimbursable dollars of the insurance claims. It now has become more costly for a patient to pay for continuing outpatient care than to receive care in a hospital, which is clearly a more expensive form of care. It is the financial reimbursement mechanisms that influence the level and type of care being given to the chronically mentally ill person. This type and level of care is not necessarily the most appropriate nor the most needed.

Bassuk and Gerson (1978) believe that the role of the newly administered antipsychotic medications on a large scale during the mid-1950s complemented the external political pressures toward deinstitutionalization. Pressure began to mount from humanitarian groups concerned with the custodial and maintenance approaches being used in place of active treatments for seriously mentally ill persons. Pressure also was mounting from state legislatures protesting the financial burdens being imposed on state budgets by the hospitals. Courts were beginning to require the states to upgrade their hospital facilities, but money to upgrade the existing facilities and improve psychiatric services was not allocated.

Which factors primarily influenced the vast deinstitutionalization of the state hospitals is still being debated. Most analysts contend that the use of antipsychotic drugs revolutionized the management of psychotic patients in America and made the community mental health system a political and policy reality. Antipsychotic drugs alone probably would not have brought about the radical transformation of care for the mentally ill that occurred. Even prior to the widespread utilization of antipsychotic medication, open hospitals were reporting that their patients appeared to do dramatically better, showing less chronic and troublesome behavior. Both Scull (1976) and Mechanic (1969) agree that the arguments that suggest that the introduction of the drugs to treat psychosis was the necessary precursor of deinstititionalization merely reinforce the medical point of view that insanity will one day be cured with the right medication. While antipsychotic medications were a factor in the changing system of care, the drug innovations alone were not the rationale for deinstitutionalization policies.

The Federal Initiative

NIMH was extremely successful in its primary mission of stimulating training, research, and service programs. The number of professionally trained mental health workers grew impressively. Outpatient facilities expanded rapidly, and in less than ten years, the influence of NIMH was felt across the entire system of mental health services. Patients, benefiting from new drug therapies and open hospital policies, were now leaving the hospital to be maintained in the community. Outpatient, aftercare, and rehabilitation services now were needed (Levine, 1981). In 1955, a working coalition had been formed consisting of the professional leadership of NIMH, the leadership of the psychiatric profession, university and medical school personnel who had been receiving NIMH training and research support, and several lobbying organizations such as the National Mental Health Association. With support from the American Medical Association and the American Psychiatric Association, Congress passed a resolution to provide for an "objective, thorough, and nationwide analysis and reevaluation of the human and economic problems of mental illness." The study was conducted by the Joint Commission on Mental Health and Illness, a nonprofit corporation financed in part by the pharmaceutical company Smith, Kline and French. Its task was to analyze and evaluate the needs and resources of the mentally ill in the

United States and make recommendations for a national mental health program. The Joint Commission's trustees included representatives of the American Medical Association (AMA), the American Psychiatric Association, the American Psychological Association, the American Association of Psychiatric Social Workers, the American Hospital Association, the American Nursing Association, and the National Education Association. The commission itself was composed of thirty-six representatives of professional and lay agencies, covering a wide spectrum of interests and perspectives. The American Legion provided funds which went towards the distribution of the final report (Foley, 1975).

In 1961, the Joint Commission published its summary volume, *Action for Mental Health*. The Commission's report has been severely criticized for its essential thrust, which was to revitalize the state hospital system. The report proposed limiting the size of institutions to prevent the worst abuses of custodial neglect. And despite its recognition for the need for extensive outpatient services on a continuing basis and stressing the value of preventative services, the Commission's focus was the care of the severely mentally ill and the need to upgrade state hospitals to a therapeutic level.

NIMH personnel, however, continued to press for a more radical approach—the creation of a community-based mental health system of services apart from the hospital. A new and powerful political constituency was being formed that would successfully influence the direction of service delivery. This constituency consisted mainly of the very professionals recently trained through NIMH funds who now were interested in going into private, fee-for-service practice. These bright, young professionals were clearly cognizant of the benefits and financial advantages that would be awarded to them if continuous federal funds for programs and services were provided for the treatment of mental illness. They had become the nation's major source of mental health providers.

NIMH's phenomenal growth was largely due to a highly organized planning effort. The legislation for the new community mental health centers (CMHC) did not develop as most national policy does. Rather than building incrementally or piece by piece from earlier programs and policy attempts, an entirely new approach was formulated (Foley, 1975). NIMH had been carefully shaping Congressional sentiment as well as generating and disseminating knowledge to form a solid groundwork for its future plans. The NIMH advocates convinced President John F. Kennedy, who was interested in developing a major new initiative in mental health, that the Joint Commission had been wrong in focusing on improving mental hospitals. A brand new community-based system throughout the nation was an idea whose time had come.

Again, several forces came together to reorient the treatment approaches for the mentally ill. Kennedy became the first president in America's history to discuss the issue of mental illness and mental retardation and state the need for a national policy. President Kennedy's own sister was developmentally delayed; thus his concerns were both personal and political. After the Joint Commission made its report to Congress, President Kennedy called for a "bold new approach" to the problems of the mentally and developmentally handicapped. Stressing the economic and psychological burdens that family members undertake, Kennedy emphasized the need to develop preventive programs that recognized the relationship of retardation to poverty and mental illness to unhealthy environmental stresses and educational and cultural deprivation.

Kennedy went much beyond the Commission's recommendations for system improvements. He set as his goal the halving of the institutionalized population and establishing a nationwide, community-based mental health treatment system. Kennedy called for the development of comprehensive community mental health centers which would have all of the services necessary to ensure a continuum of treatment close to the patient's home. Kennedy recommended a mechanism for federal funds to be used to help establish the centers, but the major proportion of their funds were to come from local and state sources, health insurance, and other third party payments. Kennedy's advisors anticipated that funds from the institutions would be diverted into the centers' budgets as the institutionalized population decreased. Congress endorsed President Kennedy's message and passed the Mental Retardation Facilities and Community Mental Health Centers Construction Act of 1963. Congress would appropriate funds to the states for the construction of a new type of facility. Each state would develop a plan with designated "catchment" areas—geographic units that would serve between 75,000 and 200,000 people. These federal funds were authorized for construction and could not be used for personnel to staff the new programs. Also, the administrative regulations issued by the United States Public Health Service required that each center, in order to qualify for federal funds, must provide five essential mental health services. These included inpatient care; outpatient care for adults, children, and families; partial hospitalization; emergency care and consultation; and education. Added to these five essential services were five "additional" ones suggested to complete the comprehensive center idea. These suggested services included specialized diagnostic services, rehabilitative services, precare and post-discharge services for state hospital patients, training, and research and evaluation.

While the existing state hospitals in many cases could have provided most of the five essential services necessary to become eligible for CMHC funds (or expanded their services minimally to meet the requirements), state hospitals were ineligible for CMHC dollars. The infusion of federal funds was for new facilities construction. The Hospital Improvement Program (HIP) and In-Service Transition grants that state hospitals could apply for were small, consisting of less than 10 percent of the CMHC funds.

By 1965, plans from all fifty states had been submitted requesting funds for CMHCs. Lyndon Johnson, now President, was influential in bringing about the passage of the Medicare entitlement as well as resisting the AMA's opposition to providing federal funds for staffing grants in the CMHCs.

From the earliest stages, the NIMH leadership attempted to increase their options and flexibility in dealing with the various state mental health programs. By supporting administrative policies that permitted them to provide mental health dollars directly to local sponsors of the CMHCs, they began bypassing the state mental health authorities. Presumably, NIMH's intention was to bring about innovation and creativity into the designs and implementation plans of the CMHCs. Bypassing the state mental health systems, NIMH hoped to avoid the well-known delays and conservatism of most large state bureaucracies and the mental health authorities. In retrospect, however, this approach segregated the community-based mental health programs from the state hospitals and led to a fragmentation and separation of the component parts of a system that many mental health patients must traverse.

Again in retrospect, the effort to build a comprehensive community-based mental health center system in America has turned out to be woefully inadequate. While the CMHC Act called for a diversity of services and attention to the particular needs of each catchment area, the result has been fragmentation of services, poor coordination of programs, and a seeming inability of the states to plan for and find funds to support an adequate array of services.

An even larger failure, however, was the failure of the CMHC legislation to recognize that patients living outside of a state hospital (a total institution) would need a broad spectrum of services that must be provided *within* the community. These needs go beyond the traditional mental health service delivery system and included housing, medical care, income, vocational training, transportation, job supports, and recreational services, most of which had been previously provided inside the institution through the state-funded hospitals (although admittedly not sufficiently). Finally, the last serious problem with the "bold, new approach" was that the other major health care policy developments—Medicare, Medicaid, Supplemental Security Income (SSI), Social Security Disability Insurance (SSDI), and the Veterans Administration Benefits Programs—were providing inconsistent incentives to the community-based mental health efforts and were not well coordinated with the deinstitutionalization efforts. By 1985, the total appropriation nationwide for these five programs was in excess of $120 billion.

Medicare was enacted in 1965 as Title XVIII of the Social Security Act and became operational July 1, 1966, with 18 million aged enrollees. Medicare is a health insurance program that works to cover in-hospital costs for general and surgical care of those over the age of sixty-five. However, it is ineffective in providing psychiatric care. There is a 190-day lifetime limit on the days of inpatient care in a psychiatric hospital that will be covered by Medicare. A patient must leave the hospital for at least sixty days after using 150 days of the first admission (regardless of the medical diagnosis or prognosis) in order to remain eligible for the remaining sixty days of eligibility that may become necessary later in life. This might been thought to be an incentive to encourage the use of outpatient services and other hospitals. But if a psychiatric patient is not hospitalized, and is treated as an outpatient in a doctor's office or a clinic, then there is a severe limitation on the costs of services that are reimbursable. Maximum yearly payments for outpatient visits could total $250 in 1986, a ceiling that has not been raised since 1965, although the costs of medical care have increased more than 70 percent during that time. This amount of money usually covers only a few visits to a psychiatrist and is totally inadequate for the chronically mentally ill. This situation also encourages professionals to hospitalize their elderly patients who may not need such services. Medicare is a $65 billion national program, yet only a small percentage of these resources go into mental health care, despite the rapidly increasing mental health service demand among the elderly (Hastings, 1986). The Medicare legislation provided strong incentives toward placing the elderly in general care hospitals, since the federal government, rather than the states, would pay for those costs. The reference point for choices regarding the mentally ill person's treatment has become the bureaucratic regulation, not the person's state of health or capacity to function. Long-term outpatient care, the very thing needed by most of the seriously mentally ill, and the problem about which the CMHC legislation should have been concerned, is extremely difficult to obtain with Medicare funds.

Medicare, Medicaid, and SSI regulations all favor the expansion of private, profit-making facilities (Brown, 1985) such as nursing homes.

In 1976, 85 percent of the Intermediate Care Facility (ICF) patients and 86 percent of the Skilled Nursing Facility (SNF) patients were reimbursed by Medicaid (Glasscote et al., 1976). Hardly any mental health clinic services, partial hospitalizations, or private households' care expenses were covered. Medicaid support of nursing homes rather than the usually more beneficial placements in halfway houses, group homes, or apartments has severely limited the housing options for the mentally ill. Of the estimated 900,000 institutionalized chronically mentally ill, 700,000 are in nursing homes, and 150,000 are in state hospitals (National Plan, 1980).

The availability of federal programs to pay for services to sick and disabled persons has had a profound impact on the locus of care of the seriously mentally ill. From 1969 to 1973, the number of persons sixty-five or over with psychiatric diagnoses in nursing homes grew from 96,415 to 193,000. The state hospitals lost a corresponding number of patients. This has been called "transinstitutionalization" and reflects a shift in the locus of care but not necessarily a qualitative improvement in the care provided.

Policies determining SSI disability payments require that the sums be reduced by varying amounts if a person is institutionalized in a facility which could be covered by Medicaid. They are also reduced if a person receives Medicaid or any state support. If a person lives with a family member, benefits are reduced by one third. And SSI money may not be used to pay for any publicly funded facility such as a halfway house or group home. Thus, SSI money is usually used by patients to pay rent in a boarding and care home, perhaps the least therapeutic living arrangement for most mentally ill persons. So, what was hoped to be a national policy of coordinated mental health services became an uncoordinated, overlapping "nonsystem" of services with a multiplicity of local government units and private agencies all taking a piece of the responsibility pie for health, mental health, education, welfare, housing, employment, transportation, jobs, recreation, and criminal justice. With this confusing and complex array of services, specialists, and programs, it is not surprising that the most seriously mentally ill and the most needy were the persons who most frequently found the cracks and gaps in between the uncoordinated care components.

It is almost an adage in the human services administration literature that when no single organization has the primary responsibility (or a defined, insured, reimbursable mechanism) to provide a particular service, that service will not be provided unless there is an increased demand from clients with the ability to pay for it. The seriously mentally ill rarely have the ability to demand improved services for themselves, nor do they have the ability to pay for the services they need. These two factors remain as the major reasons why this population is still one of the most underserved in our country.

Declining Support from the Federal Government

Implementing a community-based mental health system across the nation met with resistance. However, Congress continued to renew the CMHC Act legislation between 1965 and 1970. Services for alcoholics and drug abusers were added. In 1970, Congress authorized increased funds for services to children. But President Richard Nixon's administration opposed both the CMHC concept and the increased expenditures for research and training in mental health. In 1975, President Gerald Ford vetoed an act extending and revising the CMHC Act. Congress overrode the veto and authorized even more funds for children and the elderly. Also in 1975, the Health Planning Law was passed, requiring each state to delineate its system of services and emphasizing planning for each of the geographic health service areas. This suggested a continued commitment to mental health services by the legislative branch of government, but the federal "presence" for the support of the mentally ill had begun an inevitable decline.

Problems were becoming omnipresent on the landscape of the mental health scene. Fragmentation of responsibility, lack of clarity, and failure to define a coherent policy for the seriously mentally ill were becoming obvious (Levine, 1981). These issues were blatantly reported in the Comptroller General's Report to Congress, entitled "Returning the Mentally Disabled to the Community," published in January 1977. As the Comptroller reported, there were 135 federal programs operated by eleven major departments and agencies all involved in deinstitutionalization; eighty-nine of those were within the Department of Health and Human Services. The many jurisdictions led to confusion and poor coordination. Furthermore, there was still no central federal initiative to link these programs together and no centralized focus to implement the aftereffects of deinstitutionalization.

Another Bold Approach: The Community Support Program

NIMH now had to respond to the multitude of criticisms and did so by sponsoring a conference on community living for the mentally disabled. Another "new approach," to correct the deficiencies of the last new approach, was being framed by Turner, Stone, and TenHoor

(1977). The Community Support Program (CSP), a pilot demonstration initiative launched in 1977 by NIMH, was one response. The goal of the program was to promote the development of local systems, defined as "an organized network of caring and responsible people committed to assisting a vulnerable population meet their needs and develop their potentials without being unnecessarily isolated or excluded from the community" (NIMH, p.2). The premise of this approach was threefold. First, NIMH knew that the needs of the chronically and persistently mentally ill go beyond the traditional boundaries of the mental health system and cross over into other health and welfare agencies. Second, NIMH knew that it had become necessary to encourage local communities to make a long-term commitment to these people and that much of the cost was not third-party reimbursable. Third, NIMH knew that there had to be a clarification of the lines of responsibility from the local community, through the state governments, to the federal government. The CSP guidelines described additional needed services that included case identification, outreach services, assistance in applying for entitlements, crisis-stabilization services in the least restrictive environments, a spate of psychologically rehabilitative services, sheltered living arrangements, medical and mental health care, backup support to families and friends, mechanisms to protect clients' rights, and opportunities for involving community members to participate in the planning of the service delivery system. The problem was eloquently articulated and solutions well defined. However, funds were minimal and there was little money used as an incentive to bring about the necessary interagency collaboration. CSPs relied primarily on voluntary coordination mechanisms to promote resource sharing, joint planning, and continuity of care. Formerly independent and autonomous agencies, already facing funding cuts, were now expected to work toward formalizing inter-organizational linkages with one another. This would be difficult under the best of circumstances, but in the field of mental health, confusion over which agency or jurisdiction was formally responsible for the seriously mentally ill had not been clarified since the time when the state hospitals had first opened their doors and let their patients out into the community. With little funding and even less authority, CSP never really had a chance to bring about the developmental framework envisioned. Tessler and Goldman (1982) suggest that without financial leverage points to induce local agency collaboration, the system's development goals may be unattainable. They also make the point that it may not be feasible to attain community-wide interagency coordination around the target population of the seriously and persistently mentally ill. A formal mental health service delivery system that sees the chronically mentally ill as only a small subset of the aggregate human service clientele (though an expensive subset that uses a disproportionate share of the services and resources) is not likely to refocus its attention and/or restructure its functioning for this group. Rose (1979) contends that the CSPs were doomed from the start. He questions how the framers of the CSP concept could have expected the state mental health departments, which had continuously proven their inability to coordinate and plan services, to foster an effort bringing about a substantial change in the manner in which they conducted their business.

President Carter's Commission on Mental Health

A major problem underlying the efforts to bring about coordination and decrease fragmentation among the service components seems to be the lack of any specific authority to oversee such accomplishments. In 1977, shortly after his inauguration, President Jimmy Carter expressed his interest in mental health issues by establishing the President's Commission on Mental Health. The composition of the Commission was selected to achieve, in addition to expertise in mental health issues, a balanced representation of gender, race, ethnic, and professional background. Unlike the Joint Commission in 1955, these Commissioners were not representatives of professional organizations.

The Presidential Commission reported its results in 1979 and a Health, Education and Welfare (HEW) Task Force was formed to make legislative recommendations to Congress. The report was somewhat critical of NIMH and its inability to adequately plan and deliver a unified psychiatric services program. However, the resulting law eventually passed by Congress, the Mental Health Systems Act of 1980, did not depart significantly from most of the recommendations of the past. The variety of reforms adopted by Congress were the ones supported by the professional leadership that had been influencing the development (or lack of it) of the nation's mental health policy.

The summary report to the President neither detailed the many criticisms of existing practices nor the role the governmental programs were playing in the perpetuation of some of the existing problems. Nor did it evaluate alternative suggestions or conduct any cost benefit analyses. Rather, it reported out a series of general, pragmatic recommendations based on the value that mental health care of high quality and reasonable cost should be available to all who need it. The Commission noted that the demand for mental health services may be as large as 15 percent of the population. They were concerned with the huge outlay for physical medical expenses in comparison to the mental health expenditures and wanted to redress the inequities for those suffering from mental disorders. The Commission discussed the problem of the crazy quilt of public and private financing of the services and supported insurance reimbursements for psychologists, social workers, and nurses with advanced degrees. They also discussed the need for national health insurance legislation while protecting the freedom of choice concept (so important to the self-interest of providers).

The report had a strong emphasis on the concept of the underserved, particularly children, adolescents, the elderly, and racial and ethnic minorities. Thus, while the report was somewhat critical of NIMH and its inability to plan and deliver a unified plan of high quality comprehensive psychiatric services, the recommendations were very much in line with NIMH's own policy statements describing the need for more funds for training, research, and service programs. The report seemingly did not even consider the problems that the reimbursement formulas for federal aid to the states had in causing the major failures surrounding "dollars following the patients" in the deinstitutionalization process. It did not examine the problems local and private sector agencies have in providing community-based services to the clients now returning to live in the community. And most disappointing was the fact that the report did not differentiate the problems and needs of the seriously and chronically mentally disabled from others who may need mental health care. The Commission did not confront the major policy issues related to the care of the seriously and persistently mentally ill in America. Once again, an opportunity was lost to truly examine the needs of seriously mentally ill persons in America. Once again, suggestions for better coordination and planning took the place of problem definition and analysis. Once again, a narrow, clinical lens was used to examine a complex problem that needs a wide angle lens for a thorough and adequate analysis.

The Commission did support new initiatives in prevention, which perhaps was the most innovative thinking done. But the hope for improved coordination of state mental health plans with other health plans developed through the Health Systems Agency planning process was not based on a realistic understanding or analysis of the problems of the mentally ill, many of which need to span both health and mental health agencies in order to improve the quality of the lives of seriously mentally ill persons.

The Mental Health Systems Act of 1980

In October 1980, Congress passed the Mental Health Systems Act. This legislation authorized the continuation of funding for the community mental health centers as well as an additional $260 million in spending for new initiatives through 1984. Special emphases were to be given to the most vulnerable and dependent groups of the mentally ill, including children, the elderly, and the seriously and chronically mentally ill. The act also called for attention to the needs of the rural and minority population. The legislation followed most of the the Task Force's recommendations. It clearly reflected the swing away from federal control and toward more state involvement, a direction started with President Nixon's administration. Most of the reforms suggested by the Task Force were the ones supported by the mental health professionals' leadership that had been influencing the development (or lack) of the nation's mental health policy for the last twenty years. While the Mental Health Systems Act still mandated federal grants, it also initiated a partnership with the states. Its major themes included community-based mental health services that were comprehensive, flexible, organized, funded, and coordinated with other health, related social support, and welfare services. Other major themes called for restructuring federal/state/local involvement and participation in the orchestration of mental health services. The act also strengthened requirements related to planning and accountability and mandated the negotiation of "performance contracts" as a condition of federal funding. Roles and responsibilities were to be specified clearly (Wagenfeld and Jacobs, 1982).

The Mental Health Systems Act Repeal

It is perhaps ironic that as legislation was finally passed that might have for the first time created a unified system of mental health services in the United States, Ronald Reagan was elected president on a platform that called for a substantially reduced federal presence. When President Reagan signed the Omnibus Reconciliation Act of 1981, he repealed the Mental Health Systems Act. In place of twenty-five separate Health and Human Services programs, each with separate funding and regulations, this new legislation streamlined these programs into seven block grants for the states to allocate as they saw fit. The Alcohol, Drug Abuse and Mental Health Block Grant provided funds to the states to establish and maintain programs for the mentally ill and substance abusers and for the promotion of mental health. In line with the President's philosophy of "new federalism" (really a return to states' rights), the block grant approach minimized reporting and accountability to the federal government. The purpose of the consolidation was to give the states the flexibility to develop programs most relevant to their own needs as well as flexibility in the use of funds, thereby improving efficiency. There is little evidence to support the notion that when the states take over the responsibility for funding social welfare programs in their communities that they are particularly generous or innovative. In fact, Magill (1979) found that most of the state's decisions to fund social welfare programs get left behind since decisions to build roads, highways, construction, and public services have stronger political support. Furthermore, these issues usually have stronger lobbyists (and political contributors) whose support can be extremely influential at the local level.

The Omnibus Reconciliation Act

The implementation of the Omnibus Reconciliation Act represented an important trend reversal of expanded federal services and support for community mental health. The block grant approach, which leaves the responsibility for the delivery of mental health services once again at the local level, will have profound effects on the service delivery system in the next decades. Historically, federal programs have come into being when state and local governments have not adequately met health and human service needs. The withdrawal of federal support for mental health services raises serious questions about continued program direction. If states and localities are willing and able to take up the slack left due to the loss of federal funds and the programs remain under public sponsorship, the changes might not be too significant. But this is unlikely. A much more likely scenario is that community mental health centers will be forced to look for additional reimbursements, either through patient fees or third party insurers, and then the most vulnerable once again become the least likely to be served.

Wagenfeld and Jacobs (1982) suggest that difficult social problems often become "medicalized" as theories shift from social structural definitions to more personalized and individual deficit models. If mental disorders become relabeled as solely problems of the brain—as opposed to problems exacerbated by poverty, unemployment, and racism—it would be logical to see an increase in hospitalizations and a return to a dominant medical model for care. The Reagan administration changed funding priorities for research and training from the social sciences to behavioral and biological sciences.

The National Institute of Mental Health has begun a major reorganization and streamlining of its operations and has provided greater organizational visibility for the Institute's support of basic brain and behavioral science research. Research is emerging as the institute's major mission and the form of research is mostly biomedical (Frazier and Parron, 1987). NIMH recently announced priorities in basic research on schizophrenia and the major affective illnesses. Much of this push has come from the vigorous lobbying effort from the National Alliance for the Mentally Ill, a newly formed self-help and advocacy group of family members of seriously mentally ill persons. This group has been critical of NIMH's past efforts and contends that NIMH has forgotten the most seriously mentally ill and has moved away from the most promising areas of research—the biochemical theories of mental disorders.

New Populations of Underserved Mentally Ill

The increasing numbers of mentally ill who are homeless has become a disturbing trend in America. The American Psychiatric Association's Task Force on the Homeless Mentally Ill estimated that between 25 and 50 percent of the homeless suffer chronic forms of mental disorders. Of particular concern also are the "new chronically mentally ill" who are young, severely disabled individuals who rarely if ever have been hospitalized. The "system" of mental health care that exists is infrequently used by this population and many service providers admit to not liking this population, with their chronic problems and often counterculture life styles. NIMH, along with private granting agencies like the Robert Wood Johnson Foundation, has begun funding research and demonstration projects that will attempt to design strategies for resource usage that will concentrate more effectively on the needs of the newly diagnosed people with mental and addictive disorders.

Children and adolescents are another category of persons traditionally underserved. Only recently have clinicians begun to seriously address the problems of depression among children. New research is also identifying an alarming increase in suicide among adolescents as well as beginning to study the long-term, psychological damage sustained from child abuse, sexual abuse, and incest. Previously, these problems had been denied or minimized.

NIMH has most recently taken a leadership role in developing comprehensive strategies to address the mental health consequences of those affected by acquired immune deficiency syndrome (AIDS). There are known neurological complications associated with the

HTLV-III virus in the spinal cord and the brain, bringing these patients logically under the NIMH umbrella. And NIMH has already begun to address the issues of patient care, including the obvious emotional stress brought on when AIDS is first suspected, the depressions associated with the illness itself, and the monitoring of mental dysfunctioning of the patient, his or her family members, and friends. NIMH is also taking the lead in governmental efforts to reduce the spread among high-risk populations.

While NIMH has continued to provide leadership and has been influential in maintaining some mental health progress, the Reagan Omnibus Budget Reconciliation Act consolidated the community mental health centers' allocations into block grants, halved NIMH's budget and reduced its staff proportionately. It remains to be seen whether NIMH can continue to maintain an active role in improving the programs and services for the seriously mentally ill while it is called upon to take on other tasks and its very identity may be subsumed into the National Institutes of Health.

Recent Initiatives

While the Reagan legacy has halted the flow of new money from the federal government into state and local community mental health programs, mental health legislation continues to shape the form and functioning of the service delivery system. In May 1986, Congress enacted the Protection and Advocacy for Mentally Ill Individuals Act. This legislation developed from an investigation of the conditions in state mental hospitals conducted by the Senate Subcommittee on the Handicapped in 1984. Again, serious physical abuses and abject neglect of patients in institutions were documented. The law, P. L. 99–319, provides funds for protection and advocacy services to persons with mental illnesses in residential facilities and aids in the transition from residential to community placements. While no new rights are created under the law, the act provides for services to protect existing state, federal, and constitutional rights. Funds appropriated under this act were distributed to every state, with a minimum allotment of $125,000.

The 99th Congress also approved a law making substantial improvements in the Supplemental Security Income program. Senator Dole and Representative Bartlett wrote into law a federal policy that permitted benefits to be paid to disabled people, including mentally disabled people who work despite a severe impairment. Prior to this legislation, all disabled SSI beneficiaries determined able to earn $300 a month or more lost their eligibility for disability benefits. A diverse coalition of groups supported this bill. Senator Dole stated that this legislation was a response to "the desire of persons with disabilities to obtain both a measure of economic independence and dignity . . . . Employment is the key factor in the successful integration of disabled adults into community life."

Perhaps surprisingly, the 99th Congress expanded both the mental health services covered under Medicaid and the number of people with mental health needs who can become eligible for Medicaid coverage. New provisions included case management services that became a new optional service which states may choose to provide under their Medicaid plans. States may elect to target case management services specifically and exclusively for chronically mentally ill individuals. Congress also passed legislation permitting states to offer home and community-based mental health services, including day treatment, psychosocial rehabilitation, and clinic services in lieu of general hospital inpatient services. Now, community services can be provided as an alternative to general hospital inpatient care for mentally ill people of all ages who are covered by Medicaid. This amendment represents the first time Congress has recognized day treatment and psychosocial rehabilitation services as appropriate Medicaid-reimbursable services. The Medicaid reforms also attended to a tragically ironic problem of the homeless. Many states denied the Medicaid claims of the homeless, contending that the federal government prohibited coverage of a person without a permanent address. By definition, this eliminated the homeless! Congress clarified its intent by amending the Medicaid language to insure that homeless persons may not be denied Medicaid services simply because they have no fixed address.

In 1986 a Mental Health Planning Bill was passed. This requires that each state develop and implement a state comprehensive mental health service plan. The intent is to further interagency cooperation and coordination in meeting the needs of the severely mentally ill. The bill mandates that the states establish a State Mental Health Service Planning Council, which must include individuals who are not providers of services or state employees. The services must be defined with specific attention to the "seriously mentally ill" and activities to reduce the rate of their hospitalization must be described with specific quantitative targets to be achieved. There is no meaningful penalty if a state does not comply; however, there is money to provide technical assistance to the states to develop their plans. The Secretary of Health and Human Services was authorized to develop model standards for the provision of care to the chronically mentally ill. NIMH has been authorized to provide the technical assistance to the states.

The Robert Wood Johnson Foundation

An interesting innovation in mental health service planning and delivery is the introduction of the Robert Wood Johnson (RWJ) "initiatives." The Robert Wood Johnson Foundation, a granting wing of the Johnson and Johnson Corporation, has been interested in funding demonstration projects in particular social problem areas. Most recently, the focus has been on the problems of the seriously mentally ill. In 1985, the foundation funded twelve cities to provide medical care to the homeless. In 1986, the foundation developed a request for proposals to specifically fund citywide innovative efforts that significantly improve the *system* of care for chronically mentally ill people. Several important issues need to be underscored. First, here is an attempt by a private corporation to alter the system of care of the mentally ill. Historically, families have had the primary responsibility for such care, local and state governments have had the titular responsibility for their care, and the federal government has had spurts of responsibility. This is the first time that a private, nonprofit corporation decided to use its money and considerable influence to affect social policy in the area of the mentally ill.

Second, the foundation clearly prescribed system changes as a prerequisite for funding. The request for proposal required that the demonstrations be citywide and go beyond the traditional mental health organizational boundaries. The foundation required that traditional mental health systems join with housing agencies, vocational rehabilitation agencies, social welfare agencies, and federal entitlements to form a unified, coordinated system of care. Interestingly, this conceptualization is similar to the NIMH/CSP ideology, but this time, money would be forthcoming to plan for and fund the newly designed system.

Third, the Robert Wood Johnson initiative brought about changes in federal policies. The eight cities that were awarded the RWJ demonstration projects would have the option to waive normal Medicaid rules so as to improve services available under Medicaid for individuals served by the project. To provide the applicant cities further incentives, one hundred Section VIII Rent Subsidies from the Department of Housing and Urban Development (HUD) would be awarded to the cities selected by the Robert Wood Johnson Foundation. Now a private corporation was conceptualizing the needs and problems of the chronically mentally ill, suggesting strategies for improvement and offering money to the cities willing to change their existing operating system. It remains to be seen whether this new private initiative will succeed where other public initiatives have failed. In terms of policy development, this may represent an entirely new approach in the privatizing of the mental health system. While the mental health system may recently have been characterized by an increase in contracting out services—using private providers and private insurance systems while the public presence has dramatically decreased—the privatization of the planning and funding by non-profit corporations is indeed a novel approach to a seemingly intractable problem.

Cutbacks and Decreasing Expenditures

The Balanced Budget Act of 1985, also known as the Gramm-Rudman-Hollings Bill, has most recently had a direct impact on mentally ill people. In an effort to reduce the huge federal budget deficit, automatic cuts were to be enacted if the Congress and the President were unable to enact a budget that would meet a previously specified deficit target. In 1986, cuts of 4.3 percent were made under this procedure. Only Social Security programs were exempt from the across-the-board domestic cuts. Virtually none of the programs of crucial importance to the mentally ill were exempt from the across-the-board cuts. In Fiscal Year 1987, Congress enacted spending reductions and increased revenues through the tax bill. In fact, mental health spending increased somewhat in FY 1987 with the funding of the Protection and Advocacy system, increases in the Community Support Programs, money for the elderly and the homeless, and continued support for NIMH training.

Future Policy Issues

Social policy analysts like to conceptualize social problems from a trio of levels; usually they think about all three at the same time. Micro, mezzo, and macro level analysis, while at times confusing, is an appropriate framework for the analysis of the problem that has beset the seriously mentally ill in America. Following John Talbott's conceptualization (Talbott, 1988: pp. 13–23), the following discussion looks at patient care (micro level); economic issues (mezzo level); and systems (macro level).

Patient Care

The tragic irony regarding seriously mentally ill people is that while we have not discovered the etiology or definitive treatment for schizophrenia, major affective disorders, and other severe and chronic mental illnesses, we do know a lot more than we currently are putting into practice. We know what works best for most mentally ill people and yet in most communities those approaches are not used, primarily because they are not available. Most clinicians now agree that a combination of medication, psychotherapy and counseling, with support services in the community, is the most successful form of intervention for most seriously mentally ill persons. Using psychoeducational approaches with mentally ill clients and their families also has been proven to be an effective intervention strategy. Designing a comprehensive spectrum of services based in the community, one that ensures continuous, well-coordinated services, also works. Providing each client with a case manager, who links together services and entitlements and provides each client access to needed, high-quality hospital programs to stabilize or restabilize a person, works. Accurate and current assessment and reassessment of each client's treatment plan also significantly assists a client's rehabilitation. We know what to provide. But just knowing what to do has not turned into action in most communities. As the locus of care has shifted from the state hospital (a single institution under state auspices) to the plethora of community facilities and agencies (under private and public auspices), the point of responsibility has been diffused and no one system is responsible for the mentally ill client nor is any one seemingly willing to assume that responsibility.

Economics

Most mental health experts agree that the money has not followed the patient from the hospital to the community, nor has it been increased in sufficient proportion to the rising costs of care and treatment. Some mental health pundits have concluded that some states proceeded with removing patients from state hospitals without regard for need or resources available. Tragically, some states removed the funds and left the patients; others removed the patients and left the funds. As of July 1985, twenty-two states were under federal court order to improve their mental health systems. Clearly, the federal initiatives and federal dollars dried up, and new money and state and local initiatives to replace those dollars did not take place.

Economic discrimination against the mentally ill continues to exist, as is apparent in the reimbursement schemes. Current inefficient and woefully inadequate patterns of funding favor inpatient over outpatient care, hospitalization over prevention, acute care over chronic care, and more restrictive placements over less restrictive—in flagrant disregard of most clinically acceptable practices for successful interventions. And the reimbursement mechanisms that do exist are extremely difficult to find; the rules are difficult to obey and eligibility requirements almost impossible to comply with. The trends to save money (i.e., prospective pricing, pro-competition initiatives) work against those with chronic, episodic, long-term illnesses where the need is for intensive, long-term, comprehensive, continuous care.

The System

Again there is a great deal of agreement as to the most important system problems that impede the seriously mentally ill from obtaining the services they need. First and foremost is the severe fragmentation of the psychiatric delivery system (or what many call a "non-system"). The many layers of federally funded programs (like the Veterans Administration and its hospitals and the Public Health Service); mixed funded community mental health centers; state hospitals, alcohol, and drug clinics; county hospitals; community for-profit hospitals with psychiatric wards; general hospitals with free-standing clinics; rehabilitation centers; transitional day treatment programs— all exist without being coordinated and often with little cooperation among the components.

And that is just the psychiatric, or mental health component. Seriously mentally ill people need housing options, pre-vocational and vocation training programs, welfare, and entitlements. This array of elements does not function as a system should. It does not move easily with the mentally ill person as his or her needs change. It does not anticipate upcoming needs nor successfully adjust to changing circumstances. And not only is it not functioning well today, the changing demographics of the county foretell even more severe lacks.

A large cohort of young adults are now maturing and entering into the high-risk range for the onset of many serious mental illnesses. These young people for the most part are not tolerant of traditional mental health services in which they play a passive, dependent "patient" role. Most have only spent brief stays in psychiatric hospitals and have not acquired the institutional dependencies of many of the older mentally handicapped patients. And as the population of the United States ages, with the expected proportionately higher incidence and prevalence of mental illnesses among the elderly, it is likely that there will be even more shortages of nursing home beds, funding for home care programs, and services for this new vulnerable population.

NEW CONSUMER AND ADVOCACY ACTIVITY: ITS EMERGING INFLUENCE

Advocacy models that developed during the 1960s to assist the poor and the disenfranchised to help themselves have recently been used among the consumers of mental health services. Citizen participation became a mandate within all federally funded planning projects and innovative demonstration projects sprouted up along the paths of citizen action programs (CAP) and model cities. Civil rights were being expanded rapidly to minority groups and women. Legal cases were being argued and being won that increased the protections and rights of the developmentally disabled and some cases had implications for the mentally disabled.

During the 1970s, self-help and empowerment models began to emerge. Clients/consumers/patients began to organize themselves in an effort to secure needed services that they felt professionals could not or would not provide. The self-help ethos includes a resistance to things being done *for* the self-help group members. Self-help mutual aid relies on the indigenous knowledge of its members and their situations. The theory of self-help also includes the belief that when people help themselves by joining together with others who have similar problems, they feel empowered; they become able to control at least some aspects of their lives.

For the mentally disabled, a group often thought to be unable to advocate for itself, self-help groups have taken on several different dimensions. Primary consumer groups such as GROW, Mental Patients' Liberation Front, the National Mental Health Consumers Association, and the National Alliance of Mental Patients are organized to support and share common experiences among the participants, to assist others in similar circumstances, and to improve the services and programs for themselves and other mentally ill people. Recently, many of these groups have become politically active and are lobbying for increased mental health funding or for specific pieces of legislation related to mental health services, the homeless, and against employment discrimination.

A new self-help group, the National Alliance for the Mentally Ill, has had a remarkable growth in less than ten years. These self-helpers are family members and friends of schizophrenics, manic depressives, and other seriously mentally ill persons. This advocacy group has its common ground in that most of its members have lived or are living with a seriously mentally ill family member. They have developed literature on the etiology of schizophrenia and have become an active national organization with state chapters across the United States. They are now concerned with revising the curriculum and training of mental health professionals as well as altering the research agenda of the National Institute of Mental Health to include a more biological/psychogenic focus. Other groups, such as the Mental Health Association, the American Civil Liberties Union, and the Mental Health Law Project, are also active in advocacy activities on behalf of the mentally disabled, although they often focus on a particular concern or policy issue.

These groups and their activities have been successful in increasing the public's awareness and sensitivity to the problem of mental illness. Spector and Kitsuse (1973) discuss the natural stages and historical development of a social problem. They suggest that in order for a "problem" to become a "social problem," a consciousness must develop among a critical mass of people. This alerting of the populace attracts attention and eventually political interest, with subsequent legislative, administrative, and policy action. In many areas, this model seems accurate. Recent attention to the problems of sexual abuse, child abuse, and battered women has resulted in increased money and improved services.

The story for the serious and persistently mentally ill, however, is different. The problem is well known and well documented and the consciousness has been raised. Yet in most cases, the situation for this group of people has not been demonstrably improved over the last half century. Some even contend that the outcome of the vast deinstitutionalization movement has resulted in *less* protection and services for mentally ill people. Stigma, fear, and disinterest may have increased as the mentally ill poured out of the state hospitals and returned to "their" communities.

WHY?

That is the question that this book attempts to grapple with.

WHY do the problems of the seriously and persistently mentally ill seem so intractable?

WHY have our social policies consistently failed to assist this group?

WHY have mental health professionals (psychiatrists, psychologists, and social workers) abandoned this group while the field of psychotherapy has never been stronger?

WHY in the face of an increasing number of advocacy groups has there been so little legislative and public support for the mentally ill?

WHO has benefited and who has lost as a result of the intended and unintended consequences of the deinstitutionalization policies for the mentally ill?

3

Deinstitutionalization and the Impact of Laws on Mental Health Policy

During the last thirty years, several major changes have occurred in mental health policies, laws, and administrative procedures that have had a profound influence on the lives of seriously mentally ill people in the United States. In recent years, America has become an increasingly litigious society: one out of every fifteen people tries to settle a problem or dispute in a court of law. Mental health advocates also have turned to the courts to seek redresses to the complex problems facing mentally ill people—from protecting their rights, to insuring or restricting the use of certain treatment technologies, to forcing state and local communities to provide needed services. Laws governing mental health issues have been developing at an almost dizzying pace, affecting state mental health authorities, mental health professionals, and, of course, mentally ill people themselves and their families. The very definition of who is mentally ill and under what circumstances treatment may be provided have become the subjects of intricate legal debates.

MENTAL ILLNESSES ARE DIFFERENT

With most physical diseases, doctors diagnose the somatic manifestations of the illness, inform the patient of the prognosis, and recommend a course of treatment. Doctors, as opposed to every other group, have been awarded the right to treat illnesses, prescribe medication, if necessary even cut the body, and generally take control of the patient in an effort to heal him or her. However, with mental illness, several differences are obvious. The first "problem" is that there are no laboratory tests that can assist the doctor in his or her diagnosis. No blood or urine test is available to pronounce the patient mentally ill. Accordingly, there is a great amount of variation in the diagnosis of a mental disorder, with varying reliability between psychiatrists as to what specific illness they are seeing and what to do about it.

The second difference between medical and mental illness is that the consumers have been afforded certain rights and protections in dealing with physicians and psychiatrists. The rights of patients to refuse treatment are not absolute. A doctor may prescribe a medication that a patient does not wish to take. With a physical illness, it is the patient's right to "be foolish" and ignore the doctor's advice. However, in the field of mental health, since the patient is considered to have an illness of the mind that may be impairing his or her judgment, a court may intervene and require that the patient be institutionalized and involuntarily receive the treatment being prescribed.

Thirdly, the definitions of "being mentally ill and in need of treatment," "incompetent," "dangerous to self or others," "gravely disabled," and "obviously ill" have become legal terms debated by attorneys, not mental health professionals, and now form the basis under which many mentally ill persons are treated or released.

NEWLY ACQUIRED RIGHTS

Prior to the mid-twentieth century, there was little concern for the rights of the mentally ill. Family members could easily find a psychiatrist willing to define a person mentally ill and have him or her committed to a state hospital. Rosenhan in 1973 demonstrated the ease with which surrogate patients (graduate students saying they were hearing voices) could be institutionalized in the state psychiatric hospitals in California. The study also documented the difficulty these "patients" had in seeing a psychiatrist for treatment and, accordingly, the difficulties in proving that they were sane and ready to be released. Through legislative reform, precedent-making cases, and class action suits following the patterns of civil rights legislation, the rights of mentally ill persons have become widely protected and enforced. In 1986, the federal government passed the Protection and Advocacy Bill, insuring that every state will have a state office that has as its primary mission protecting the rights of mentally disabled people. This is a landmark in the historical march of rights for mentally ill people.

DEINSTITUTIONALIZATION AND INVOLUNTARY HOSPITALIZATION FOR A MENTAL ILLNESS

The influence of changing legal opinion on mental health treatment is clear when only one statistic is reported. Prior to 1970, 90 percent of all mental patients were committed to hospital care involuntarily and the bulk of all patient care episodes took place in mental hospitals. In the 1980s these figures changed. The intended purpose of judicial involvement in the commitment process is threefold. First, by establishing due process for the mentally ill, the individual presumably is protected from arbitrary state action that could deprive a person of civil liberties. Second, judicial overview presumably protects the community from those who are dangerous to the public. Third, judicial involvement can bring persons who are dangerous to themselves, but unaware of their need for help, into the treatment system.

DEINSTITUTIONALIZATION AND PUBLIC AWARENESS

The role or influence of social science (and research generally) on public policy is frequently debated. However, in the field of mental health policy, it is generally agreed that social scientists did influence the shape of the deinstitutionalization movement and sped the patient's rights movements. Thomas Szasz, the controversial psychiatrist, wrote several books that were widely read both by mental health experts and the public at large. His work was frequently quoted in the legal briefs of the seminal cases. His *Myth of Mental Illness* (1961) and *Manufacture of Madness* (1970) argued that the mentally ill were being labeled and then put into a coercive system dominated by psychiatrists, not because they had an identifiable illness, but because they violated our social norms and were living a different lifestyle that the dominant culture found threatening. Abominable conditions existing in mental hospitals were once again popularized in Ken Kesey's novel *One Flew Over the Cuckoo's Nest* (1962) and later made into a widely seen movie. And Irving Goffman's *Asylums* (1961) brought home the systematic negative impact that institutions ("total institutions") had upon their inmates. These influences affected the thinking of the courts and were responsible for bringing about changes in the commitment laws throughout the states.

A HISTORICAL NOTE

When the first American mental hospital opened in Williamsburg, Virginia, only a physician's signature on a slip of paper was necessary to commit a person into the institution. Ironically, it was believed then that this was necessary to ensure that paupers would not sign themselves in to "enjoy the institutional comforts." As states built institutions for the mentally ill and mentally retarded, little thought about their protection was even considered.

Cases like that of Mrs. Elizabeth Packard were common. In 1866, Mrs. Packard was committed to an Illinois state hospital by her husband. At that time, the Illinois statute allowed married women and infants to be hospitalized against their will at the request of the woman's husband (or child's guardian), without even the minimal evidence of insanity required in most other states. It took Mrs. Packard three years to subsequently win her release. She wrote a two-volume book that detailed her experiences. It is unknown how many other women were inappropriately committed. Although most actions by relatives to hospitalize their kin involuntarily were based on humanitarian concerns, some were motivated by the desire to preserve or control property (Levin, 1981). Mrs. Packard led a crusade in the mid-1860s that successfully changed the lax commitment laws in a number of states. In Illinois, after Mrs. Packard was granted a jury trial and found sane, the state passed the Packard Law in 1867, requiring a jury trial to determine lunacy before anyone could be committed to an asylum. While the intention of this law was to protect the insane from inappropriate commitment at the behest of a family member, there is some question whether the resulting criminal procedures and jury trials decreased the number of wrongful commitments. Reviewing the history of the Packard laws should give pause to those believing that the rights of the mentally ill will be insured through a rigorous due process requirement. The requirement of jury trials may protect mentally ill people from the most obvious and abject abuses, but it turns over the complexities of determining the existence and extent of mental illness to lay persons. And the experts agree that it is impossible to make an accurate prognosis for most mentally ill people. Nor can their future "dangerousness" be predicted, yet the legal process calls for such a determination to be made prior to an involuntary hospitalization, which by definition withholds a person's civil rights.

REVOLVING THEMES

As with most social problems, when solutions are not forthcoming, "new" approaches are tried again. The history of litigation and reform surrounding mental health issues has almost come full circle. As professional psychiatry developed more respect and authority, commitment laws changed. The medical model embraced by most psychiatrists provided the rationale that confinement was for therapeutic purposes, for the good of the patients, and thus that commitment laws should be relaxed. Legislators happily relaxed laws and deferred to the experts in formulating the procedures governing commitment for mental disorders. Other mental health professionals also argued for easier commitment laws, believing that the court process was traumatic to already distraught persons (and their families) and because with involuntary commitments they had greater control over their patients while in the institution.

Scheff (1966) studied commitment procedures in one state and described how in only a few minutes, a person could be involuntarily committed simply on a sworn petition of a relative or friend, accompanied by a doctor's certificate that the person was in need of treatment. Commitments could be for an unspecified length of time, with discharge being solely at the discretion of a hospital director.

DEINSTITUTIONALIZATION AND THE ATTACK ON PSYCHIATRY

In the era of civil rights for blacks and other minority groups, the Supreme Court was actively shaping a new social agenda. In 1967, the Supreme Court held that due process had to be extended to juveniles (*In re*: Gault). The court held that if a juvenile was to be confined in a state institution, the juvenile was to be afforded an attorney and all the protections of due process. In *Specht v. Patterson*, the court held that confinement of adults, even when considered to be helpful, must follow all the requirements of due process hearings.

A mental patients' rights movement slowly emerged; it provided the first critique of psychiatry coming largely from the patients themselves. Small groups of ex-patients began to assert themselves and vent their anger for being committed for what they felt to be minor "deviant" acts and began to criticize the efforts to be resocialized into an institutional life style. These groups also began to meet and form support groups that eventually developed into the various forms of self-help organizations that dot the mental health field today. During this time, litigation also was emerging, but mostly from individuals and/or professional advocates. The early cases were partly a result of the general interest in civil rights legislation and advocacy efforts from the civil rights movements.

Bruce Ennis published a book in 1972 called *Prisoners of Psychiatry*, which described his experiences as an attorney litigating on behalf of mental patients. Ennis complained about the large number of persons who were being confined and deprived of their rights without sufficient reason or adequate protections. In *Lessard v. Schmidt* (1972), a Wisconsin court held that a mentally ill person should not be denied due process of law and held involuntarily when there is little compelling interest by the state to do so. The court ruled that an allegedly dangerous person had a right to a speedy hearing, with advance notice of what expert testimony would be heard. Further, dangerousness had to be proved beyond a reasonable doubt and involuntary commitment was to be a last resort after a less restrictive environment was tried. (This standard of proof was not upheld in a later Supreme Court case.)

The logic of the courts was that the state could not deprive a person of their liberties on the basis that there is a high probability that a person *might* commit a crime in the future. Yet a psychiatrist's recommendation for involuntary commitment is just such a prediction (Levine, 1981). The assumption was that there would be potential benefit to the person confined in a mental hospital. This was finally being debated.

The courts were becoming less and less convinced that a commitment to a mental hospital was always beneficial and that minimum criteria of need would have to be established before one's civil rights could be taken away. In the Lessard case, the court insisted that the standard for commitment be interpreted to include a finding of "imminent danger to oneself or others, based on some recent act, attempt or threat to do substantial harm to oneself or another." The Lessard decision also held that no one should be held for more than forty-eight hours on an emergency basis without a finding of probable cause at a preliminary hearing. The right to counsel was also reaffirmed. Several states were changing their statutes without waiting for litigation. Massachusetts changed its laws in early 1970 so that involuntary commitment of a mentally ill person was technically more difficult and became less frequent. Indefinite commitment has now been abolished.

THE LOCUS OF CARE

As the criticism of the state hospitals continued, a new concept of "least restrictive alternative" was first articulated in 1966 in the case of *Lake v. Cameron*. Ms. Lake was a sixty-year-old woman who was picked up by the police, "wandering." She was clearly not dangerous to others and not likely to intentionally harm herself. However, her wandering often left her confused and exposed to the elements. Ms. Lake was found "dangerous to herself because she was not competent to care for herself" and was committed to St. Elizabeth's Hospital in the District of Columbia. The court recognized that she was entitled to release if another less restrictive alternative facility was available. Ms. Lake appealed the ruling. Judge David Bazelon of the Appellate Court found that the deprivation of liberty should not exceed what was necessary to protect an individual and asked the lower court to inquire about the availability of less restrictive alternatives. No suitable alternatives were found before Ms. Lake died in St.

Elizabeth's Hospital. It was not until 1969 that the courts even hesitantly began to order the states to actually provide alternative treatment facilities.

THE RIGHT TO TREATMENT

In *Rouse v. Cameron* (1966) Judge Bazelon gave the first formal recognition to the right-to-treatment concept. He held that Mr. Rouse, who had been committed to St. Elizabeth's Hospital, should either be set free or must receive adequate treatment. If Mr. Rouse was not receiving appropriate treatment, his rights were being violated and he should be released from the hospital. Judge Bazelon stated that the District of Columbia statutes provided for the right to treatment when confined to a mental hospital. Such rights could be derived from the U.S. Constitution's Eighth Amendment guarantee against cruel and unusual punishment and the Fourteenth Amendment guarantee of due process and equal rights under the law. The judge also found that inadequacy of resources was not a good enough reason to deny an individual the right to treatment. However, since no constitutional issues were decided and the language describing adequate treatment was unclear, the court ended up merely asking the hospital to make an honest effort to improve its services. Little actually changed.

Not until 1972 (*Wyatt v. Stickney*) was the constitutional right to treatment asserted. Federal District Court Judge Frank Johnson Jr. contended that when patients are involuntarily committed for treatment purposes, they unquestionably have a constitutional right to receive such individual treatment as will give them a realistic opportunity to be cured or to improve their mental condition. Going further than *Rouse v. Cameron*, *Wyatt v. Stickney*, defined a set of standards granting patients the right to privacy, mail, phone calls, and visitors. Physical restraints and the use of isolation were restricted and rigid staffing minimums were prescribed. Therapeutic labor was strictly defined so that hospital maintenance work must be voluntary and patients were to be free from unrestricted or excessive medications; weekly reviews from physicians were required.

The court gave the state authorities six months to raise the level of care to the constitutional minimum. The court also stated that the state had the affirmative duty to provide adequate transition treatment and care for all patients released after a period of involuntary confinement.

The right to treatment was also given strong support in a consent decree in Massachusetts. In 1976, a class action suit on behalf of the patients in the Northampton State Hospital resulted in a reduction of the hospital census from 475 to 50 patients by 1980. The Department of Mental Health consented to the decree and used it as leverage to obtain additional legislative funds from the state for community-based mental health programs.

Unfortunately for Kenneth Donaldson, not all states concurred. In 1975, in *Donaldson v. O'Connor*, the Supreme Court ruled that non-dangerous persons who were not receiving treatment should be released if they could survive outside of the hospital. Mr. Donaldson had spent fifteen years involuntarily in Florida's Chatahoochee State Hospital. The hospital superintendent constantly blocked Mr. Donaldson's release saying that Donaldson was uncooperative for denying his illness and refusing ECT and that his behavior was inappropriate for waging a legal battle for his freedom. Mr. Donaldson was so well versed in patient's rights law that he had an article published in the *Georgetown Law Review*. However, Mr. Donaldson was not released until the hospital superintendent retired. The Supreme Court did not uphold a lower court's monetary award to Donaldson, probably defeating a significant precedent for malpractice suits.

THE UNINTENDED CONSEQUENCES OF IMPROVED RIGHTS

The impact of much of the patients' rights litigation is still questionable. While certainly the rights of most mentally ill persons are now better protected, unintended consequences have resulted in *less* treatment for seriously mentally ill persons. It was clear that when Alabama was unable to comply with the court orders to improve the level of treatment within its institutions (as mandated in *Wyatt v. Stickney*), many patients were merely released into the community without the transitional services that were also required. Many states have abandoned the mentally ill by merely removing them from the resident rolls of the state hospitals. It is much harder to find, let alone assess, the "treatment" being provided to a mentally ill person over whom the state has technical authority when the person is living in an unlicensed board and care home or a dilapidated hotel.

THE RIGHT TO REFUSE TREATMENT

One of the first cases involving a patient's right to refuse treatment was that of *Price v. Sheppard* in 1976. In that case, electroshock therapy was declared an "intrusive treatment" and thereby not allowed against the patient's will if the patient were competent. During the same year, two cases were heard on whether the injected antipsychotic medication Prolixin was intrusive. One court found it was and thus the patient had the right to refuse it as a form of treatment; in another jurisdiction, the court held that it was not intrusive. *Wyatt v. Stickney* had previously held that patients had the right to refuse ECT, aversive conditioning, psychosurgery, or other major surgery. In 1973, in *Kaimowitz v. the Department of Mental Health of Michigan*, the court held that an involuntarily committed patient's consent to psychosurgery was uninformed and that no such patient should be subject to psychosurgery. The controversy surrounding ECT and psychosurgery left most mental health experts accepting these rulings. However, in the area of refusing the more typical treatment (i.e., antipsychotic medications), new controversies rage.

The federal court rulings in this area have not been decisive. In *Rennie v. Klein* (1979), a New Jersey District Court held that all patients who were involuntarily confined have the right to refuse medications if they are competent and if they are not in an emergency state. This was contingent upon the review of an independent psychiatrist. A 1981 appellate ruling removed the requirement of the outside arbitrator. In Utah, however, committed patients have no right to refuse such treatment under the language of the Utah commitment laws.

Perhaps the most famous case of the right to refuse treatment is the Boston State Hospital case of *Rogers v. Okin* (1979). After several years of in-hospital organizing by the Boston Mental Patients Liberation Front, several suits were filed by patients against the hospital, its psychiatrists, and the Department of Mental Health. Federal District Court Judge Joseph Tauro granted the plaintiffs their right to refuse seclusion or forcible medication, except with the express consent by themselves or their guardians, or where there was a substantial likelihood of extreme violence, personal injury, or attempted suicide. The defendants argued that a committed patient was *de facto* incompetent to decide on treatment issues and they feared that such an order would lead to a widespread refusal of medications (a situation that did not subsequently occur). The state filed an appeal on the grounds that it had a responsibility to treat committed patients and that Judge Tauro's ruling prohibited the necessary exceptions to the right to refuse treatment (Dietz, 1979). The Federal Appeals Court sent a partial reversal back to Judge Tauro in 1980. That court held that the judge too narrowly limited forced medication to cases where patients were either mentally incompetent or were prone to harm themselves or others. The essential rights of patients to refuse treatment in a wide range of circumstances, however, was protected.

In 1982, the Supreme Court returned the Boston State case to the Circuit Court of Appeals for a redetermination, since the Massachusetts law potentially provided a greater right to refuse treatment than did the U. S. Constitution.

COALITIONAL POLITICS

While earlier coalitions of mental health consumers, activists, and professionals had joined together to bring about right to treatment protections and the expansion of least restrictive alternatives, they broke apart on the involuntary commitment laws and most decidedly on the right to refuse treatment. Most psychiatrists argue that the right to *refuse treatment* would mean that a patient would be deprived of the previously won right to be *guaranteed treatment*. Psychiatrists, like other professionals, frequently resist challenges to their professional judgment from any outsider, particularly activists who are seen to be unaware and insensitive to the real plight of the mentally ill. Most professionals are likely to resist any legal infringement that would lessen their authority to practice their profession. And the right to refuse treatment issues pit the duty to protect the community against the rights of the mentally impaired. Freddolino (1982) found in his survey that most psychiatrists agreed that patients should be fully informed of their rights (even the right to refuse treatment), but many fewer were in favor of granting that right to their patients. Perhaps the abstract constitutional right is easy to concur with, but the practical implementation becomes difficult for those concerned with ward management and hospital routines. Shortages in staffing complements often result in a heightened need to manage the environment as a tight ship. There is significant evidence that even when patients are given the right to refuse treatment, few actually do. The Massachusetts Psychiatric Wards Study in 1979 found that only 12 of the 1000 patients in the study refused medication during the time of the court-ordered injunction against forced medication. Even so, the fear of disruption of the hospital's routines looms large in administrators' minds. Further, the psychiatric profession is extremely proud of its successes with antipsychotic medication to control and manage the overt symptoms of psychoses. These medications have become standard practice. The problem lies in the fact that, almost universally, patients report that antipsychotic drugs provide unpleasant side effects that may range from suppressed urination, impotence, dry mouth, and ungainly gait, to the fear of tardive dyskinesia, a side effect that may result in irreversible brain damage. Patient groups and consumer advocates disagree sharply with the professionals and family members who contend that constant medication is the most effective treatment for serious mental illnesses and that, if necessary, the force of the law must be used to keep ill people taking their medications, under supervision.

'ROUND AND 'ROUND IN THE CIRCLE

A new era is upon us now. Commitment laws are being eased as a new tide of civil rights interpretations are taking place in the context of the needs of severely mentally ill people and their families. Efforts to balance the public's interests with those of seriously mentally ill people remain in a delicate equilibrium. Citizens want to "maintain and conserve" their neighborhoods and enjoy their expected increases in property values unencumbered or threatened by the existence of residential facilities for handicapped populations or even the presence of seriously mentally ill people. The "not in my backyard" syndrome has become a potent force in limiting access to apartment units, homes, and community-based programs for mentally ill people throughout the United States. Some predict a shift towards reinstitutionalization, citing the rise in the numbers of mentally ill who are homeless and the apparent unwillingness of most neighborhoods to accept returning patients into their environs.

The laws and policies that assisted in the deinstitutionalizing of thousands of hospitalized persons from state hospitals directly into the community have resulted in additional serious problems for mentally ill persons. Their story is now pretty well understood. While patients in state hospitals, many received inadequate treatment, yet they were housed, fed, and monitored. When released into the community, few aftercare programs were there to meet them, few followup services were there to greet them, but they did find many hostile neighbors and a confusing array of nonsupport systems. Finding a place to live that they could afford in a neighborhood that was minimally tolerant was extremely difficult. The deinstitutionalized "returned" to communities that did not want them and often to families who could not provide and/or protect them. Pressure from family groups to put the mentally ill back into protected asylums has resulted in many states further easing their involuntary commitment laws.

And now a new group of mentally ill individuals, labeled "chronic young adults," has emerged, causing new headaches for mental health planners, legislators, and mental health professionals. These people, most of whom had little or no history living in state hospitals, are labeled "chronic" because of their predicted or expected future and frequent episodes of mental illness—not their chronicity of hospitalizations. These young persons often have serious substance abuse problems and are not compliant with existing psychiatric methodologies. Many refuse to be "maintained" on antipsychotic medications and often refuse treatment in group homes and/or socio-rehabilitative therapies. Their obvious illness combined with their unwillingness to conform to traditional treatments distress not only the mental health experts and the "public" who now daily see these people on the streets and in the malls, but also the families of these young people. Family members, who have remained silent sufferers for decades, now are finding a voice in the emerging self-help movements born of the 1970s. Family members began to advocate for easing the entry requirements into state hospitals and for insuring legal ways to secure involuntary treatment for their child, spouse, or other relative. The National Alliance for the Mentally Ill has been most active in this effort and claims to have successfully softened the commitment laws in many states.

THE SHIFT TO REINSTITUTIONALIZE THE DEINSTITUTIONALIZED

The Supreme Court has cautiously permitted states to ease their commitment laws. In *Addington v. Texas* in 1979, the court allowed for commitment by "clear and convincing evidence" of 75 percent certainty, rather than the previously held "beyond a reasonable doubt" evidentiary level of 95 percent certainty. Critics had argued that in the area of mental illnesses, the criterion of "beyond a reasonable doubt" is unrealistic. While it may become easier to get into a state hospital, there is not much evidence that the services inside have improved much. In 1980, mental health advocates in Massachusetts were successful in passing legislation that would mandate improvements at the Northampton Hospital and insure an increased hospital budget from the state legislature. But after an initial victory, a federal appellate ruling reversed a lower court ruling ordering the state to allocate the dollars as agreed upon in the consent decree with the Northampton Hospital. The appeals court set aside the injunction that prohibited the state legislature from reducing the hospital budget. Thus, the improvement of inpatient care for the mentally ill was once again competing against other more popular legislative initiatives.

Improved services and patients' rights are costly and as budget cuts come, it is expected that the implementation of even the few court-ordered minimum standards will not occur. It is likely that financial considerations will block the broad implementation of recently won patient rights and service innovations. There is a sad irony in the fact that now, due to budget cuts, the community-based care system is insufficiently funded. It was originally the presumed financial savings that prompted the institutional reform movement in the first place, since hospitalization was deemed to be too costly. It seems that society is just unwilling to spend substantial amounts of money on mentally ill people, whether they live in the hospital, the community, or the streets.

POSITIONS AND INTERESTS

New advocacy efforts must be designed to reframe the issue and restructure the service delivery system for the seriously mentally ill in our nation. Advocacy groups of consumers, family members, and concerned volunteers must unite their efforts and forge a coalition that has as its primary strategy the improved quality of life for this most vulnerable population. As long as the advocates disagree with one another, choose competing strategies to win their cases, and bicker about the priorities, those with mental illnesses will languish untreated and poorly cared for. It is unjust for America to leave unserved these most needy of its citizens.

4

Dollars Following Clients?
The Influence of Financing Methods on Mental Health Care

The form and structure of financial arrangements have always influenced the form and structure of social welfare programs and the resulting quantity and quality of the service delivery system. This is particularly apparent for the services provided (or not provided) to people who suffer from serious and persistent mental illness. As a collective responsibility developed towards the mentally disabled, social policies began to emerge based on the value premise that the individual suffering from a mental disorder and/or his or her family members should not be solely responsible for the financial burdens and costs of treatment.

Historically, physical health care plans and protections have developed prior to mental health services. Now there are multiple sources of funding in the public sector at the federal, state, and local levels, as well as a rapidly changing system of private payment mechanisms. In 1963, the federal government for the first time delineated the array of services which it deemed necessary for the mentally ill and, more importantly, for which it would reimburse states that provided them. The Community Mental Health Centers grew out of this federal initiative and the states and local communities began providing essential services to the mentally ill. As services became more targeted (examples include programs for children and adolescents, the young adult chronic, the homeless, the elderly, the special needs of women and minority groups, and substance abusers), numerous funding sources sprung up in attempts to finance this growing system of services.

ENTITLEMENT AND CATEGORICAL PROGRAMS

The largest amount of federal funding for mental disabilities comes through the entitlement programs: Medicare, Medicaid, SSI, SSDI, and Veterans Administration Benefit Programs. Nationwide, in FY 1985, these programs cost $120 billion. Entitlement programs as a policy formulation were clearly delineated from "welfare" programs. Whereas welfare programs were means tested and eligibility had to be established through financial need, entitlement programs were granted to beneficiaries based on their membership in a category (e.g., elderly, disabled). Today, however, entitlements exist in a variety of forms and this distinction is becoming blurred. Entitlements now exist for specified services to eligible persons, such as the benefits provided under Medicare and the Veterans Benefits. However, entitlements also exist for individuals who need income for basic needs, as under SSI and SSDI. And there are hybrids of these entitlements such as the Veterans Administration, which gives medical services to entitled persons and also provides disability income to support individuals.

Mental Health's Payment Structures

The largest single payment source for personal mental health expenditures in the United States comes from private funds (35%); another 25 percent comes from federal sources, 28 percent from state and local sources, and 12 percent from private insurance plans. This is on a total mental health revenue base of $30.5 billion. Sixty-three percent of the mental health dollars go for institutional care. The total cost of benefits in the federal programs (Medicare, Medicaid, Social Security, and the Veterans Administration) in FY 1985 was in excess of $120 billion.

Medicare

The first major federal program to insure against the costs of physical illness protected the elderly over the age of sixty-five. Medicare was enacted in 1965 as Title XVIII of the Social Security Act and became operational July 1, 1966, with 18.1 million enrollees. Medicare is a health insurance program that covers all reasonable expenses for general medical and surgical care for the first sixty days of inpatient hospitalization minus a deductible of $540 (1988 figure) in each benefit period. Sixty-one to ninety days of inpatient care is covered with a $135.00 coinsurance payment. When more than ninety days of care is needed, a beneficiary must draw from his or her sixty-day lifetime reserve. A coinsurance amount of $270 is deducted for each reserve day (U.S. Ways and Means Committee Report, 1988). One hundred days of skilled nursing care are also covered and after the first twenty days, a $68 daily coinsurance is deducted. Medically necessary home care is covered as are hospice services for dying, elderly patients.

While psychosis was ranked the sixth highest volume category in the diagnosis related group ratings, with a mean hospital stay of thirteen days, the coverage for mental illness is inadequate to protect individuals against the high costs of psychiatric care. The program severely limits the benefits for psychiatrically disabled persons. The Medicare legislation limited reimbursable psychiatric care to a 190-day lifetime maximum on the days of inpatient care in a psychiatric hospital. Furthermore, a patient must leave the hospital for at least sixty days after using up the first 150 days of the first admission (regardless of the medical diagnosis or prognosis) in order to remain eligible for the remaining sixty days of eligibility that may become necessary later in life. This might have been thought to be an incentive to encourage the use of outpatient services and other general hospitals, but if a psychiatric patient is not hospitalized and is treated as an outpatient in a doctor's office or a clinic, there are severe limitations on the reimbursable costs of the outpatient treatment. The maximum yearly payments for outpatient visits was $250 in 1986, a ceiling that had not been raised since 1965—even though the costs of medical care increased more than 70 percent during that time. This amount of money usually covers only a few visits to a psychiatrist and is totally inadequate for chronically mentally ill people. This situation also encourages professionals to hospitalize their elderly patients who may not need intensive and expensive services.

Medicare is a $65 billion national program, yet only a small percentage of those resources go into mental health care, despite the rapidly increasing mental health service demand among the aging (Hastings, 1986). The Medicare legislation provided strong incentives toward placing the elderly in general care hospitals, since the federal government, rather than the states, would pay for those costs. The reference point for choices regarding the mentally ill person's treatment has become the bureaucratic regulation, not the person's state of health or capacity to function. Long-term outpatient care, the very thing needed by most seriously mentally ill people and the problem with which the Community Mental Health Centers' legislation should have been concerned, is extremely difficult to obtain with Medicare funds.

1988 Medicare Amendments   To demonstrate the solidarity of the mental health constituency, a lobbying coalition was formed made up of the National Alliance for the Mentally Ill, the National Mental Health Association, the American Psychiatric Association, the American Psychological Association, and the National Association of Social Workers. They lobbied successfully for an increase in the National Institute of Mental Health's budget for research and may have been influential in bringing about many of the improvements to the current Medicare program enacted.

The new law increases maximum Medicare reimbursements for outpatient mental health services from $250 per year up to $1,100 (with the beneficiary still subject to a 50 percent matching copayment). "Medication management" visits to a physician are now covered without limit. These benefits will help mentally ill people defray some of the costs of their illness and outpatient clinic costs.

Catastrophic Health Insurance Approved   The Catastrophic Health Insurance Bill was passed in the second session of the 100th Congress in June 1988. It has important provisions and additional protections for mentally disabled people. This insurance provides protection against the high health care costs for elderly and disabled people who are covered by the Medicare program. It also covers the costs of prescription drugs, including those used to treat mental illness, after a deductible has been met. Beginning in 1991, Medicare will pay 50 percent of the cost of outpatient drugs after payment of a $600 deductible. This rate will increase to 80 percent in 1993.

Nationally Mandated Mental Health Insurance Benefit   A Minimum Health Benefits for All Workers Act, introduced in 1987 by Senator Edward Kennedy and Representative Henry Waxman, was passed by the U. S. Congress in the spring of 1988. This legislation guaranteed the provision of a minimum package of health care benefits to 24 million workers and their families who currently have no insurance coverage. All employees would be required to provide health insurance, which must include a prescribed minimum health care benefit package to individuals employed more than 17½ hours a week. Originally, the bill did not have a mental health benefit included, but a coalition of mental health advocates and organized labor pushed for the inclusion of this benefit and were successful in having the bill amended to include mental health benefits. The final version of the bill included mandated insurance for inpatient care up to forty-five days a year and a provision in which two days of partial hospitalization treatment could be substituted for one day of inpatient care, both with a 50 percent copayment. Outpatient coverage also was included with unlimited visits to a physician covering diagnoses, prescriptions, monitoring, and other case management activities. Twenty visits a year to a mental health professional for psychotherapy and counseling are also covered, with the patient paying 50 percent of the costs.

Nationally mandated health insurance benefits are a relatively new concept. Only thirteen states had laws mandating mental health care, so this law will significantly improve the availability of mental health care for millions of people. Also, the coverage of partial hospitalization and outpatient care is a significant step in shifting the long held priority toward inpatient care.

Medicaid

Medicaid was enacted in 1965 as Title XIX of the Social Security Act. Although it was a federally assisted health care insurance program, it differs substantially from Medicare in design, funding provisions, scope of service inclusion, and eligibility requirements. It is a selective program (rather than an entitlement program), providing medical benefits to certain low income individuals and families. The program provides assistance to those persons eligible to receive cash payments under Aid to Families with Dependent Children (AFDC), and SSI for the aged, blind, and disabled. Each state administers the program's eligibility criteria.

In 1982, through the Omnibus Reconciliation Act, a Medicaid waiver for home and community-based services was offered to the states to fund a variety of community services as an option to those who would need institutional level care, such as the mentally ill. In 1988, revisions in the Medicaid laws required states to continue coverage for severely impaired persons who had lost their eligibility for cash assistance because of earnings from work. It also prohibited states from denying benefits to persons without permanent addresses (thus making the homeless eligible for benefits). However, in 1988, 28 percent of the Medicaid funds were spent on inpatient care, 14 percent on skilled nursing facilities, 29 percent on intermediate care facilities, and only 4.8 percent for outpatient hospital care and 2 percent for clinic services (Ways and Means Report, 1988). Thus, over 70 percent of the expenditures were being used for institutional-based care. The amount of Medicaid expenditures makes it the largest single mental health program in the United States. Medicaid provides financing for a variety of mental health services, both mandatory and optional. However, Medicaid excludes reimbursements to individuals between the ages of twenty-two and sixty-four who are living in "Institutions of Mental Diseases" (IMD). A psychiatric hospital or nursing home in which more than 50 percent of the residents are diagnosed with a primary mental disorder is considered an IMD. Thus, Medicaid for non-aged, mentally ill adults is limited to inpatient services in general hospitals or to nursing homes that are not IMDs. (The intention of this provision was to insure nondiscrimination.) Mandatory mental health benefits under Medicaid include inpatient services in the psychiatric unit of a general hospital, limited outpatient services, physician services, and skilled nursing care facilities for those over twenty-one. Congress recently clarified its intent regarding community-based care under Medicaid in order to prevent the federal agency which runs Medicaid (the Health Care Financing Administration) from tightening the rules for the programs so as to exclude certain people with mental illness. In 1988, HCFA ruled that any community living arrangement, such as a group home, where four or more persons who have mental illness live together, can be classified as an IMD. The change in this rule meant that hundreds of thousands of mentally ill people living in community settings would suddenly find themselves ineligible for essential Medicaid health and mental health benefits.

A coalition of the National Association of State Mental Health Program Directors, the National Mental Health Association, and the Mental Health Law Project convinced the House and Senate committees to reinstate the policy of applying the IMD rule only to large facilities. As an amendment to the Catastrophic Health Insurance Bill, Congress defined an IMD as being limited to a "hospital, nursing facility or other institution of more than 16 beds that is primarily engaged in providing diagnosis, treatment, nursing care, and related services." This clarification, one hopes, will result in broader state development of mental health packages that include personal care services, case management, rehabilitation, and clinic services. And while Medicaid will not cover the costs of room and board, it will now cover virtually all other community care costs for persons with severe mental illnesses, if the state chooses to make the best use of the federal Medicaid options.

Social Security Disability Insurance

The SSDI program was enacted in 1956 to pay wage related benefits to insured workers under the age of sixty-five. It is financed through taxes on employment. SSDI provides cash assistance for living expenses and could have been an important help in maintaining a seriously mentally ill person in the community. However, to be eligible, a person must have a work history, which becomes a significant obstacle for many mentally ill people who have never successfully maintained the required employment history. The purpose of this disability progam was to replace income lost when a wage earner becomes disabled. Mental impairment is a part of the disability definition, but it must be medically determined and expected to last for not less than 12 months. There is an intitial five month waiting period after the disability has been determined and then it must be reviewed at least every three years.

In FY 1987, of the 1,570,000 disability determinations considered, 64 percent were denied. Fifty-seven percent of the initial denials were reversed by administrative judges at the Office of Hearings and Appeals of the Social Security Administration. Twenty-three percent of the disability benefits go to mentally disabled people (U.S. Ways and Means Report, 1988).

Supplemental Security Insurance

SSI was enacted in 1972 as an amendment to the Social Security Act and superseded the federal programs for the aged and disabled. Payments are made to the needy aged, blind, and disabled, without consideration of previous employment. Financing comes from federal general revenues, as opposed to the trust fund arrangement for SSDI.

SSI recipients must meet income test eligibility requirements on a monthly basis. They must have less than $1900 in assets to be eligible. If a person is living in another person's household or receiving support and maintenance in-kind, the $354 monthly allotment is decreased by 33 percent. If a person becomes a resident in a public institution, he or she will become ineligible for SSI unless the institution is Medicaid approved. Recent legislative changes have permitted SSI payments to persons in publicly operated community residences serving no more than sixteen persons or defined as public emergency shelters. Legislative changes in 1987 included the provision that SSI benefits will be continued for three months even if a person is residing in a psychiatric facility (if a physican certifies that the stay will not exceed three months). This is to help people maintain their living arrangements in the community.

If eligible, the state must provide the client with vocational rehabilitation services. Individual benefit allotments are measured against a basic payment level and are determined in relation to other existing income sources, family status, and living arrangements. The Ways and Means Report (1988) estimated that 26 percent of adult SSI recipients have some mental disorder. Anderson (1982) makes the point that the very signs and symptoms of mental disorders frequently prevent an ill person from establishing eligibility for the benefits to which they are entitled (Anderson). Two and a quarter billion dollars is spent each year on disability benefits, with 11 percent of the total benefits being specifically designated for the mentally ill.

The Reagan administration pushed for tougher standards to determine SSI eligibility. Thousands of persons were taken off the SSI rolls and many became involved in lengthy appeal processes. Again, the mentally ill are rarely able to find their way through the complexities of an adjudication hearing to secure their benefits. Anderson (1982), a psychiatrist, recommends that mental health professionals become advocates for their patients and understand that persistent, careful documentation of case records is now crucial and a minimum requirement for a mentally ill person to maintain his or her disability status. He reminds his professional colleagues that "there are hundreds of thousands of mentally disabled Americans who could be enjoying a higher degree of personal dignity, freedom, normalcy, and treatment in the least restrictive environment, if only they were provided the necessary assistance to establish their eligibility for disability benefits" (Anderson:298).

The Veterans' Administration

The Veterans Administration, which consolidated all of the other veteran programs in 1930, spends $8.3 billion each year on medical care benefits. Mental health benefits are substantial, with extensive inpatient, outpatient, and long-term care services.

Block Grant Funding

The Omnibus Budget and Reconciliation Act of 1981 created nine block grants to the states for a variety of services. The successor to the Community Mental Health Centers Act and the Mental Health Systems Act is the Alcohol, Drug Abuse and Mental Health Services Block Grant. For FY 1985, a new funding formula was designed based on each state's population and per capita income. Block grants funds also were earmarked (incidentally, almost a contradiction in terms) so that at least 5 percent of the allocation went for new and expanded alcohol and drug abuse services for women and at least 10 percent for mental health services for severely disturbed youth, both unserved and underserved populations.

The largest block grant to the states is for social services. This is the successor to the Title XX entitlement program. One of its primary goals is to prevent institutionalization, by providing a range of community-based services. State discretion in defining the service package is extremely broad.

STATE FUNDING FOR MENTAL HEALTH SERVICES

As described in Chapter 1, the states historically have been responsible for the majority of mental health care costs. The state governments have functioned in a variety of roles, including those of planner, regulator, provider, and funder. Each state may develop its own laws governing the rights of patients, involuntary commitment procedures, and definitions of who is mentally ill, "gravely disabled," or "obviously ill." The state then must define what spectrum of services will be offered and reimbursed. Each state also regulates its standards of care through provider arrangements, contracting out to private vendors, and direct appropriations to state-administered and/or state-run programs and facilities. Arrangements differ dramatically among the fifty states, with the result that a seriously mentally ill person in Hawaii may receive substantially different treatments and services than a person living in Virginia. The legal and policy variations between states may result in a situation in which two people with the same diagnosis and prognosis may receive radically different treatment. One may be involuntarily institutionalized in a state hospital and the other may be treated at home with a mobile community support team. The fiscal policies and facilities availability determine the form and level of care, not what is most therapeutic.

Each state has a mental health "authority" or state agency that is responsible for the distribution and allocation of mental health funds. These departments are accountable to the state legislature, governor, local and federal governmental units, providers, consumer groups, advocates, and recipients of the services.

State funding patterns have been changing due to the influence of federal programs, insurance mechanisms, and the decreasing numbers of persons living in the state hospitals. In 1984, Mazade and Glover estimated that approximately 80 percent of the funds for financing state mental health departments came from state general revenues. Approximately 70 percent of the funds are utilized for state institutional operations, with the remainder going to community-based care. A complex problem for many state mental health agencies is that state dollars may go into services of importance to mental health care, but over which the state mental health agency does not have jurisdiction. The city may regulate housing vouchers; social services regulates welfare benefits; vocational rehabilitation is run by another state agency, so that the coordination of services becomes a huge task of the state mental health departments. Increasingly, state mental health agencies are spending more and more time coordinating their services with a broad array of organizations, including education, corrections, welfare, substance abuse, child welfare, adult protective services, and public health departments.

THE STATE HOSPITALS

A controversial issue that is being debated in all of the states is the relationship between and resource flow from the state mental health authorities and their state hospitals. As has been documented earlier, the resident population in state hospitals has declined precipitously and yet the majority of resources still being spent in state hospitals remains at approximately 70 percent of the states' mental health budgets. The state hospital now plays a different role in the mental health system. It is now focusing increasingly on legal status patients (misdemeanants as well as the criminally committed); the multiply and severely handicapped; and those considered to have serious behavior management problems for whom there is no appropriate community-based facility available and/or in which the surrounding community is publicly opposed to having such patients in the neighborhood. The private sector has been reluctant to develop programs and services for these people, either because financial incentives have been insufficient or because it has been traditionally the responsibility of the public sector to care for the most difficult patients.

Some contend that the continuing use and expense of the state hospitals is primarily due to the slow development of residential alternatives. Some blame the state authorities for their less than enthusiastic attempt to obtain the necessary state funds to support such alternatives. Others suggest that there is little professional interest in this chronic population, and there are relatively few studies documenting "success" with this group. Others blame the "public" and cite almost universal opposition to the siting of such community-based, residential facilities "in my backyard." Another key factor is the needed cooperation of general hospital psychiatric units to accept both voluntary and involuntary patients. Hospitals are concerned with the low reimbursement rates of the Medicaid patients as well as the increased staffing demands that seriously mentally ill patients may need. Hospitals worry about the mixing of poor chronic patients with the privately insured (known as paying) patients. And they fear that insufficient aftercare programs in the community may prolong the hospital stay in an acute ward (even if the patient is able to pay the costs). Legal issues related to *ex-parte* orders, the need to establish guardianship, and the patient's right to refuse treatment all act as disincentives to private sector participation.

Talbott (1980) has written extensively about the inherent problems of maintaining high-quality state hospital programs. He notes that the upkeep of the physical facility and the difficulty in recruiting and maintaining staff are only two of a series of problems plaguing state hospitals. Other issues include the lack of coordination with other mental health system components and outpatient services, the myriad governmental and bureaucratic procedures, the emphasis on cost containment rather than quality, and the intense political atmosphere in which state hospitals must function. While most agree that there will always be a need for some secure hospital beds for seriously mentally ill people, the debate rages as to how much and how quickly a successful downsizing of the state hospital should be. If the community care system does not develop, the press to reinstitutionalize the mentally ill again in state hospitals will occur. Several states have already begun relaxing their involuntary commitment laws to more easily institutionalize the huge numbers of homeless chronically mentally ill. Clearly, this is not a good solution and will only once again drain money away from the development of an adequate community-based service system.

PRIVATE SECTOR FINANCING

During the last thirty years, there has been an increase in private insurance and other private third-party payment systems, such as Health Maintenance Organizations and self-insured corporate plans. Unions most recently have been actively negotiating for inclusion of mental health coverage within their fringe benefit packages—often as an extension of their basic medical care coverage. Muszynski (1983) surveyed 300 plans providing psychiatric coverage and found an overwhelming bias toward in-hospital psychiatric treatment, despite evidence that this level of treatment for many persons is unnecessary and is always more expensive than outpatient alternatives. Many employers are now attempting to cut their mental health costs by providing aggressive employee assistance programs, encouraging preventive use of outpatient programs, and offering a variety of "wellness" plans.

SOME POSSIBLE CHANGES

A new approach to financing mental health care, called capitation financing, could have profound implications for how care will be organized and provided. The expansion of health maintenance organizations throughout the country and the federal government's experimentation with Diagnostic-Related Groups (DRGs) as a method of introducing prospective cost planning to the Medicare system have led this trend. Talbott and Sharfstein (1986) suggest that capitation methods of financing have become a viable alternative for chronically mentally ill persons who already use a variety of outpatient services. Harris and Bergman (1988) contend that the HMO system may be just the necessary tonic to repair the fragmentation omnipresent in today's service delivery system.

PROBLEMS WITH FEE-FOR-SERVICE APPROACHES

Physicians, consumers, planners, and advocates alike agree that a good treatment system for persons with serious mental illnesses must have a continuum of care, be individualized to the specific client, and be comprehensive across several social service agency boundaries (Bachrach, 1984). But current fee-for-service system reimbursement mechanisms do almost none of the above. Fee-for-service systems reimburse a single clinician (or treatment facility) for a specific unit of service at a previously defined rate. Separate interventions that are time-limited, compartmentalized, and discrete make billing and accountability easy. That approach, however, does not work well with the problems facing persons with serious and chronic mental illness.

CAPITATION FINANCING

Capitation is a tax levied against each person; a certain amount per head. In the context of health care, capitation means an insurance system in which fees are set *in advance* of the service provided and a set fee is established which covers all services for an individual for a given period of time. The Kaiser Permanente Medical Clinics are perhaps the best known and largest capitation system in the United States. An established benefit package is designed with a comprehensive array of services within it. Each individual who signs up for the program is entitled to that array of services. By defining reimbursements in terms of individuals, rather than units of service, better planning and updated knowledge about the patient population is possible. The Kaiser programs have been able to remain competitive by focusing on early diagnosis of illnesses and a health promotion strategy that decreases costs. As opposed to private practice and other fee-for-service arrangements, practitioners in capitation systems do not receive additional reimbursements for each separate and additional service rendered. If a capitation system were applied to persons with persistent mental illnesses, incentives would be altered to provide the most clinically appropriate level of care individually tailored to each patient, thus better meeting each client's needs, rather than following the reimbursement biases of hospital and institutional-based care.

There has been very little empirical testing of a capitation system for mentally ill people, although the idea has caught the imagination of some. One program, Community Connections in Washington, D.C., has had several years of experience. They have enrolled 150 chronically mentally ill patients and assumed complete responsibility for stabilizing and maintaining these clients in the community. Seventy-five percent of the enrollees were from St. Elizabeth's Hospital (the District of Columbia's sole public mental hospital) while another 25 percent enrolled directly, with the patient's family purchasing the program's case management services for a set fee on a yearly basis. All of the enrollees had "failed" using the traditional modes of treatment previously offered.

The first evaluation of the program clearly demonstrated that Community Connections could provide case management services, necessary inpatient care, unreimbursed Medicaid and Medicare costs, personal care costs, and nonreimbursed medications for an average cost of $15,093. This compares with $47,000 for a similar client using the traditional community mental health services, and $82,000 for a client remaining in St. Elizabeth's Hospital (Harris and Bergman, 1988).

The broad range of services available through the capitation system includes individual and group therapy, supportive counseling, financial management, crisis intervention, a housing program with placement options, crisis beds, a supervised vocational program, a drop-in center, transportation services, and an inhouse medication clinic (Harris and Bergman, 1988). Aggressive case management successfully kept the inpatient days per person extremely low and thus kept the dollars in the community. Of course, there are some risks associated with a capitation program for mentally ill people. The deflection from inpatient services to community-based alternatives that will reduce costs is predicated on the establishment of adequate alternatives in the community. Crisis intervention programs, 24-hour on-call availability of clinicians, flexible work schedules for the case managers, and intensive crisis beds must be in place before a capitation program can begin.

Some also fear, as many did with the original health maintenance organizations (HMOs) for medical care, that doctors or staff persons will "ignore" the needs of the client if the care would be expensive in an effort to save the HMO money. Peer review mechanisms have been successful in the capitated medical programs. However, consumers of medical care HMOs can merely change insurance carriers if they feel that their care has been insufficient. Consumers of mental health HMOs, however, may need some system of evaluation and advocacy to insure that the services they are receiving are adequate and of high quality.

THE NEED FOR COMPREHENSIVE SERVICES

Alternatives to the HMO approach continue to stress the need to bring the multiple funding sources together into a single stream aimed at providing a comprehensive array of services to meet the complex and differing needs of seriously mentally ill people. It is believed that in order to provide a comprehensive set of mental health services, health care, social services, housing, transportation, and vocational rehabilitation agencies must jointly coordinate their efforts and structure a single budget stream for chronically mentally ill people. Reallocation and redirection of funding must stimulate the development of new programs such as crisis care, respite care, residential alternatives, and psychosocial rehabiliation to reduce the need for inpatient episodes. Cross-agency arrangements must be centered so that as a mentally ill person traverses the "system," an array of services follows him or her. Currently, the bias toward inpatient care in the public and private sectors encourages an overutilization of the inpatient service component (Hastings, 1986) and an underutilization of the existing outpatient services. This pattern has led to delay in the development of community-based alternatives (since the costs of inpatient care have remained high and new money has not been forthcoming) and thus for many, no services at all.

THE INPATIENT PROBLEM

Of the estimated two million seriously mentally ill persons in America, 300,000 are in nursing homes, 200,000 are in state hospitals, 150,000 are in shelters or living on the streets, 300,000 are living in boarding and care homes or foster homes, 200,000 are living independently, 800,000 with families and relatives, and 26,000 in prisons and jails (Torrey, 1986). From 1969 to 1973, the number of persons sixty-five or over with psychiatric diagnoses in nursing homes grew from 96,415 to 193,000. The state hospitals lost a corresponding number of patients. This has been called "transinstitutionalization" and reflects a shift in the locus of care, but not necessarily a qualitative improvement in the care provided (Rose and Black, 1985; Brown, 1985).

Examples of policies that work in opposition to successful deinstitutionalization abound. For example, Supplemental Security

Income disability payments require that dollars be reduced by varying amounts if a person is institutionalized in a facility which could be covered by Medicaid. They are also reduced if a person receives Medicaid or any state support. If a person lives with a family member, benefits are reduced by one third. SSI money may not be used to pay for any publicly funded facility such as a halfway house or group home, unless it has fewer than sixteen residents. Thus, SSI money is usually used by patients to pay rent in a boarding and care home, perhaps the least therapeutic living arrangement for most of the mentally ill.

So what was hoped to be a national policy of coordinated mental health services became an uncoordinated, overlapping nonsystem of services with a multiplicity of local government units and private agencies all taking a piece of the responsibility pie for health, mental health, education, welfare, housing, employment, transportation, jobs, recreation, and criminal justice. With this confusing and complex array of services, specialists, and programs, it is not surprising that the most seriously mentally ill and the most needy are the persons who most frequently find the cracks and gaps in between the uncoordinated care components. As mentioned earlier, it is almost an adage in the human service administration literature that when no single organization has the primary responsibility or authority (or a defined, insured, reimbursable mechanism) to provide a particular service, that service will not be provided unless there is an increased demand from clients with the ability to pay for it. The seriously mentally ill rarely have the ability to demand improved services for themselves, nor do they have the ability to pay for the services they need. These two factors are the major reasons why this population continues to be one of the most underserved in our country.

NEW ADVOCACY EFFORTS

New advocacy efforts are needed to improve this situation. The National Alliance for the Mentally Ill (NAMI) has launched a national lobbying effort to change the financing arrangements to the care of the seriously mentally ill. The National Association of Social Workers, along with the National Mental Health Association, were active in the successful passage of the Kennedy-Waxman bill that provided a national minimum mental health insurance program for employed people. NAMI has been attempting to get legislation passed that would provide family caretakers with benefits when they care for seriously mentally ill relatives at home. NASW is examining approaches for mandated national health and mental health coverage for all employed persons. New coalitions are forming and new advocacy strategies are being designed. The next chapter examines the new advocacy movement and its potential influence on improving the lives of seriously mentally ill persons in the United States.

Changing Models of Advocacy

Advocacy has become a term that almost every group and organization interested in bringing about change uses to describe a significant portion of its activities. Social service organizations interested in helping others, obtaining resources for themselves and their clients, or changing laws and policies frequently describe their actions as advocacy. The term has powerful symbolic meaning (see Milner, 1986) even though it has rarely been carefully defined or even precisely described.

Professional social work has claimed the term advocacy as uniquely its own and even prescribed its use in its Code of Ethics as a requirement of successful practice (see NASW Code of Ethics). It has been defined as a "core activity of social workers" and one that distinguishes social workers from other helping professionals. Social work advocacy emphasizes activities designed to defend the rights of others, champion the cause of the less fortunate, find just resolutions to injustices (both real and perceived), and ensure improvements (read changes) in social service systems. And while social work has rarely defined its methods or detailed the boundaries of the activities that encompass advocacy (see Sosin and Caulum, 1983, for one attempt), it remains a strongly held value within the profession and is continuously stressed in social work training. The symbolic content of advocating on behalf of others and bringing about organizational/systems change has strong political and moral appeal. This is particularly true in the field of advocacy for people with mental illness. The term mental illness carries with it an intense stigma, accompanied with fear and even loathing. Thus, mentally ill persons, as well as those associated with them (including family members and friends), have a difficult time advocating for themselves and often become dependent on others to explicate their cause.

NEW ADVOCACY EFFORTS

In recent years, a self-help movement has emerged in which primary consumer groups and self-help groups have gained legitimacy, power, and respect (Powell, 1987). Groups such as Alcoholics Anonymous (AA) and Adult Children of Alcoholics (ACOA) have become extremely popular and effective in using self-help models to organize the sufferers themselves to assist others as well as help themselves. However, mentally ill people as a group are still considered by most professional groups, agency representatives, bureaucrats, politicians, and even their own family members to be unable to successfully articulate their own needs and/or actively participate or be involved in the planning and implementation of the services designed for them.

Historically, patients' rights groups have formed and have been successful in winning some class action suits particularly surrounding the issues of the right to treatment, involuntary hospitalization, and, ironically, the right to refuse treatment (see Milner, 1987). Recent self-help efforts such as GROW and Emotionally Handicapped Anonymous have attempted to model themselves on the AA approach and develop support groups for mentally disabled persons. However, there has been little progress among mentally ill people *themselves* to advocate for improved services, programs, and resources. Those efforts have been mainly left to others.

ATTEMPTS AT DEFINING ADVOCACY

While the term *advocacy* has intuitive appeal and is widely written about and exhorted, exactly what it is and what it is not is rarely discussed. *Advocate* comes from the Latin word meaning to speak to a matter or issue. In contemporary use today, it has come to mean speaking on behalf of a person or issue, usually a person other than oneself.

Sosin and Caulum (1983) have attempted to more clearly conceptualize the term *advocacy* within social work practice. They cite a lack of precision and specificity surrounding the term as discussed in the social work literature. They review the different definitions of social work advocacy that span a broad range of activities. Wilson (1977) writes that advocate may mean legal counselor, spokesman, supporter, pleader, defender, protagonist, intercessor, proponent, mediator, monitor, petitioner, activator, coordinator, ombudsman, expediter, enabler, promoter, protector, instigator, investigator, and exposer.

The Ad Hoc Committee on Advocacy for the National Association of Social Workers concluded that advocates are persons who argue for, defend, maintain, or recommend a cause or proposal, or plead the cause of another (Ad Hoc Committee on Advocacy, 1969). An advocate also is expected to be a supporter, advisor, champion, and if need be, representative for another in dealing with the court, police, social agency, and other organizations (Briar, 1967). Sosin and Caulum (1983) note that the broad and variable definitions of advocacy leave social workers with no clear practice typology. In their effort to be more specific, they developed the following definition of advocacy: "An attempt, having a greater than zero probability of success, by an individual or group to influence another individual or group to make a decision that would not have been made otherwise and that concerns the welfare or interests of a third party who is in a less powerful status than the decision maker" (183:13).

This definition suggests that an advocate must clearly articulate the precise goal or change that is desired, identify the specific target capable of making the change happen, and select the strategies and activities needed to bring about that change. An important contribution of Sosin and Caulum's work is their attention to the relationship between the role and power of the decision maker and the context in which the decision may be made. They suggest that there is a rather delicate relationship between the type of change being sought, the person, agency, or organization that has the ability to make the change being sought, and the types of activities that are most likely to succeed. Understanding the elements of these relationships will assist the advocate in selecting the most appropriate strategy to bring about the desired change.

MODELS OF SOCIAL ACTION

Haynes and Mickelson (1986) suggest that as social workers moved into the political arena, three models of social action emerged: the citizen social worker, the agent of social change, and the "actionist." They note that social action activities are distinct from advocacy, but they do not explain the differences. However, they do describe the differing perspectives found among the three models of social action that social workers use to respond to the need for social change.

The citizen social worker uses the information and knowledge gained through work with individuals and groups to inform the larger society of needed programs and policies. These data are then used as evidence for the need to improve the human service system or the institutions that are impinging upon a person with a problem. Most social workers today easily embrace this form of action/advocacy and see it as their professional responsibility to act in this manner on behalf of clients.

The agent of social change has as his or her goals to achieve desirable social ends utilizing well developed and well formulated theoretical systems as a guide to action. Here social workers are active participants in an organization's political process. Social workers are involved in political action to produce change in institutional relations and policy formulation that may result in changes in the community power structure. Most social workers see this as an appropriate professional activity and usually work within their own agency structure and lobby for increased program funds, increased benefits for clients, and improved and expanded services.

The third model, that of the actionist, rejects the ideal that cooperative, rational problem solving is *always* most effective in bringing about change. The actionist operates from the perspective that political, economic, and social pressure must be won from the power structure and redistributed among the disenfranchised. This model rejects professional detachment and the insistence on societal sanction for the profession's actions. Actionists, although not opposed to cooperation and collaboration as strategies, have more often been identified with attempts to develop power; they tend to view conflict and bargaining as the best method to bring about desired change.

Just as a clinical social worker must assess a client's situation before selecting an intervention strategy, so too must a social work advocate assess the society's definition of the problem. He or she must consider the size and scope of the target population as well as the other relevant actors. The advocate examines the self-interests of the people who currently benefit from the status quo as well as the constraints and forces that are (and will be used) to prevent change. Then activities include deciding on the most realistic intervention, accurately predicting its costs (organizationally, politically, and fiscally), implementing the strategy, and evaluating the results.

AN EXAMPLE OF ADVOCACY

This example may demonstrate the complexity of the advocacy approach for social workers. An advocacy group was concerned with protecting the confidentiality of rape victims who were being counseled at a Rape Crisis Center housed in a hospital. They were protesting the practice of mailing bills directly to the insured party for medical and counseling services provided by the rape center. (The group was concerned because in many cases the female victim was not the person responsible for the medical insurance payment. In such cases, the hospital's bill would be sent to a husband or father, whom the victim may not have told about the rape.) The advocates assumed that the billing procedure was the responsibility of the hospital and thus aimed a letter-writing campaign at that target. Later it was learned that the billing procedure had been designed by the hospital's medical insurance carrier and not the hospital. The hospital was an incorrect target and should not have been the focus of the strategy if the advocates were going to bring about their desired change. Focusing on a decision maker who does not have the ability to bring about the desired change is clearly an unsuccessful strategy to achieve the goals the advocacy group seeks. And perhaps equally important, it may have damaging consequences to the reputation of the advocacy group that has expended effort and energy futilely.

Obviously no strategy, however neat, can bring about a desired change if the target selected is unable to do what is being requested (or even demanded). A crucial task in defining a problem is to discover who is primarily responsible for the continuation of the problem. Who or what (in the case of laws and policies) is responsible for the situation as it is; and who or what has the power to bring about a change? This crucial component of the problem solving process in advocacy is frequently glossed over and groups "assume" they know where the locus of control lies. Frequently, they are incorrect. Frequently, good strategies fail because the aim is on the wrong target.

DYE'S POLICY MODELS FOR SUCCESSFUL ADVOCACY

Thomas Dye (1981) describes six distinct policy models which he contends one must choose among if one is to select an intervention strategy that will succeed. The first, called the *institutional model*, focuses on policy as the output of governmental institutions. For example, an organization seeking to change a policy must know if the policy is a state policy, a county policy, or an administrative edict. After ascertaining that crucial information, advocacy efforts can then focus on the structural arrangements that are currently encouraging that level of institutional output, and change them in order to bring about structural level changes. In contrast, Dye's second model, called the *process model*, focuses on the actual details of the decision making activities. Who actually makes the decision that is of importance to the advocacy group? The question now is, who is making the policy and why is s/he doing it that way? What type of information is needed to convince the policy maker (or his or her reference group) to consider making a change? Interpersonal influencing, persuasion, lobbying and testifying at legislative committee hearings, conducting surveys, writing reports, and gathering and reporting out data are successful techniques when interventions and strategies are being designed to change decisions.

The *group theory model* sees intergroup relationships as the key to problem solving. The focus here is on interaction between political groups and the individuals with shared interests who have coalesced for political purposes. Strategies that build a strong political base of citizens are usually successful in bringing about desired change. But others see an *elite theory model* as the most accurate portrayal of American policy models for political advocacy. Elite theory views public policy as largely determined by the preferences and values of a very small and powerful governing elite. Only when this elite sees a change to be in its self-interest will change occur. Thus strategies include finding a self-interested reason for the elite to accept (or better yet support) the desired change.

The most frequently studied model among students of policy analysis is the *rational* or *efficiency model*. This model assumes that policy making is a rational and logical process. After all of the costs and benefits of every option have been calculated, assessed and considered, the best option is rationally chosen. Whether this is possible in the real world and how close analysts can come to replicating the ideal is a major debate in the field. The gap between the analysis on paper and the political realities of actually getting the needed information and implementing the "best" option is the major drawback with this model.

And finally, the *incremental model* of policy change sees public policy as largely a continuation of past policies marked only by small incremental changes that rarely change the general direction of the status quo. This model is conservative and only marginally responsive to the inequities that exist in society, but is the least risky, usually the least expensive, and the most politically expedient.

CONCEPTUALIZATION OF THE PROBLEM

While there are many models of social policy and social action in the literature, there are relatively few for the advocate. One problem is that there is a poor level of problem conceptualization for the advocate to work with. If a problem is not defined clearly, adequate analysis is virtually impossible and any resulting strategies are unlikely to be successful. Whereas the problem in the rape center example cited previously was relatively simple, advocates find that precisely defining the problem they are working on is usually much more complex. Every social problem may be understood from a variety of perspectives. The underlying cause of a social problem may be multifaceted, so that one political analysis and a different economic analysis may both be correct. Albeit, the logical strategy designed to bring about change will differ according to the perspective chosen. Every element of the advocate's plan hinges on the first step—the definition of the problem. If several advocacy groups use different problem conceptualizations, they will develop different intervention strategies that may later compete with one another and work against their main purpose.

A classic social work example may be seen in the struggle for licensing professional social workers. Many states succeeded in establishing certification or licensing for social workers at a time when private practice social work was growing and jobs in the public sector were shrinking. Thus, licensing was seen as a method to insure a high standard of professional practice and a way to protect clients. However, as the need for social workers grew in specific fields such as child protective services and corrections, licensing was seen as an impediment to recruiting needed workers (well-trained or not) and thus some people from the public sector began to oppose licensing as a restrictive hiring practice. What is the true definition of the problem? The need for improving the quality of social service through well trained and certified social workers, or the need to hire staff to conduct the crucial and often times mandated public social services required in a state? Depending on the definition of the problem and the self-interest of the group defining the issue, different positions, strategies, and interventions will be offered. Defining the major problems of people with serious mental illnesses has become a major obstacle for the several advocacy groups interested in their issues. The next chapter will explore the several different orientations that exist among those advocacy groups working with mentally ill people.

DEFINING ADVOCACY AGAIN

Robert Barker, in *The Social Work Dictionary* (1987), defines advocacy as "the act of directly representing or defending others; in social work, championing the rights of individuals or communities through direct intervention or through empowerment." Even though this NASW publication does not delineate the specific techniques of advocacy, the professional Code of Ethics (1979) notes that the social worker's primary obligation is "the welfare of the individual or group served, which includes action to improve social conditions. Therefore, a commitment to this code is a commitment to social action." Thus, championing the rights of others is a mandated activity according to the profession's Code of Ethics. The Code of Ethics also states that "advocacy is a basic obligation of the profession and its members" (p. 4).

CASE VERSUS CAUSE

Almost two decades ago, Robert Sunley published a seminal article making a conceptual distinction between "case" advocacy and "cause" advocacy (Sunley, 1970). Case advocacy is often defined as "good, old fashioned social casework." Its elements include direct face-to-face activities designed to strengthen an individual's or family's functioning and enhance their ability to solve problems, whether intrapsychic, interpersonal, socioeconomic, or environmental. Sunley added the notion that it is the responsibility of all social service agencies to look beyond their individual client or family. He contends that it is a core function of human service agencies to oppose the negative aspects that social institutions and systems have on people individually and in groups, including neighborhoods, communities, ethnic, and other groups. Learning from the experiences of clients, social workers must move from "case" to "cause" by going beyond the agency's boundaries to local, state, and national issues.

Sunley (1970) sees social casework as being comprised of four component parts: the diagnosis, the treatment plan, the treatment/intervention, and evaluation. Advocacy is similarly divided into four parts: study, planning, action, and evaluation. And while never clearly specifying the practice elements of advocacy, Sunley suggests that advocacy should be considered a separate method of practice, with its own concepts, framework, and intervention techniques.

"Cause" advocacy differs from "case" advocacy most clearly in its presumed "adversarial stance against defects or lacks in existing systems and target institutions that resist change" (Sunley, 1983:70). The focus of action is outside of the individual client and upon the system or institution that is seen as a primary stressor. This internal/external dichotomy has frequently divided the social work profession. Trained practitioners clearly know that a different knowledge base, skills, and values surround the activities of case advocates versus cause advocates, yet these distinctions are rarely explicated and practitioners are expected to cross over these lines with little training or preparation for the shift.

The National Association of Social Workers devoted an entire issue of *Practice Digest* in 1984 to the topic of advocacy, again attempting to define and delineate this elusive concept. Betty Sancier, although never quite defining her terms, contends that "advocacy in the interest of vulnerable populations for the purpose of redressing social justice has always been a part of social work. Advocacy must be practiced at the individual, issue oriented, and institutional levels" (Sancier, 1984:3). She later describes family advocacy as "social work intervention which engages the cooperative efforts of clients, staff, volunteers, and board members in the identification and assessment of those social conditions which adversely affect families and in the implementation of appropriate actions to help correct them" (p. 5).

ADVOCACY AND SOCIAL WORK

The social work profession is in a unique position to contribute to the knowledge of the effects of poverty, poor housing, inadequate education, and lack of opportunity. Yet, as a profession, social work has failed to become sufficiently involved in the planning of social programs and formulating of social policies to affect these problems. Today's social workers rarely seek, nor are they asked, to take a significant role in the development or implementation of strategies to relieve the human suffering they see daily. The macro level strategies that might effectively alleviate some of the obvious stressors in society are being designed by others (if at all).

The role of the social worker as advocate has always been problematic within the profession itself. Although social work had its beginnings in direct practice, it has always had a strong theme focused on the goals of social justice and equity. A few social workers have taken an active part in social reform efforts and some have successfully altered some of the social conditions for the vulnerable. But social work educators have been slow to put content on politics, strategies for political intervention, and social change into their curriculum (Haynes and Mickelson, 1986), and most social work agencies tend to shy away from such activities.

THE WINDS OF CHANGE

By the mid-1960s, as the American public "rediscovered" poverty, many from within and outside the profession began to criticize traditional social work casework methods. This led to a growing awareness of the limits of traditional professional methods in social work and a challenge to the role of the social worker as expert problem solver. Murray Ross's (1955) *Community Organization* introduced the concept of community practice to social workers as a "process in which community cooperation and collaboration could be built around problem solving." This approach, while well accepted among mainstream social workers, quickly was criticized as being inadequate in the face of the civil rights activities, antiwar organizing, and the developing social action models being practiced all across the nation.

Social action models interested a small but articulate sector of the social work profession. These models criticized both the intra-psychic, clinical approaches of traditional social work practice and the gentle community process models of social reform. Supporters of social action argued that social work's roots were in the community, fighting for environmental and social/structural change, not solely in intrapersonal insights. A few schools of social work took the lead in this area by developing community organization curricula and practice specializations, and eventually a distinct field of macro social work practice was developed.

Throughout the 1960s and into the 1970s, since there were jobs, money, and public support for this approach, the field expanded rapidly. Dean Harry Specht once commented that during the 1960s there was a huge field of practice called community organization and a dearth of social work literature; however, by the mid-1970s there was a huge literature in community organization but no place left to practice it.

The over-idealistic models of social activism were rapidly becoming discredited during the 1970s, and more pragmatic (and conservative) goals were again being promulgated by social workers (as well as the nation).

SELF-DETERMINATION / SELF EMPOWERMENT

Social action models with the goal of restructuring social and political institutions were slowly being replaced by "locality development" or "social developmental" models. These models used consensus rather than conflict as forms of problem solving and focused on the long-range goals of transferring to others the knowledge and skills needed for people to take on their own struggles and activities towards self-improvement. Rather than the social worker knowing best, there was the conviction that the people most affected with the problem knew the most about what changes needed to be made. This approach assumed that those change strategies that included the participants themselves would make people more aware and self-reliant and would result in the development of local experts with organizational expertise. It also assumed that the knowledge and skills that professionals had were not so difficult to share and that society would benefit if this sharing took place.

This conceptualization of advocacy, perhaps with a minor broadening of perspective, falls neatly within the social work profession's "usual" frame of reference and again aligns its practice activities with its primary activity—social casework. Placing the knowledge and skills at the disposal of the client/consumer, as well as initiating social action on his/her behalf, is the notion of empowerment that has become popular in the 1980s and perhaps is replacing the term *advocacy*, with its adversarial connotations (see *Practice Digest*, 1984).

Empowerment encompasses the notions of self-help, self-determination, and entitlement—concepts well accepted by social workers. Social workers acting as social investigator, mediator, and enabler restrain their professional activities to a rather limited range. The role of social activist and agitator was never very well integrated into American social work practice, although it had been well accepted in England (Simpson, 1978). There, social workers were traditionally expected to impart information to clients about their rights and encourage them to engage in social action towards achieving political influence.

In the United States, many social workers have been bothered by the advocacy mandate put into the profession's Code of Ethics. Their concern has centered around the issue of client self-determination. If client self-determination is always paramount in social work practice, wouldn't the scope of a social worker's activity logically stop when the interests of one client had been served? Must that responsibility expand to similar clients in the same category who may not have come forth with a common concern?

A distinction is now being drawn between "social" casework and "clinical" casework, which seems to permit many social workers to eschew the responsibilities of advocacy (and even empowerment) and return their practice to direct casework focusing on an individual client's concerns with his or her intrapsychic material. Empowerment, which in other fields entails the radical notion of political realignment of power, in social work is defined only as "a transfer of skills and knowledge . . . that will be of benefit to all" (Sancier, 1984).

THE CONFLICT BETWEEN EMPOWERMENT AND SELF-DETERMINATION: AN EXAMPLE

Another example involving the rights of rape victims demonstrates this subtle shift of emphasis occurring within the social work profession. It is well known that only a small fraction of women who have been sexually assaulted are willing to inform the police and fewer still are willing to be publicly exposed to an often humiliating cross-examination as a witness in a court trial confronting the alleged assailant. Yet when rape advocacy programs were first being developed, rape advocates and crisis intervention counselors (often victims themselves and not necessarily trained social workers) supported and encouraged each victim to remain in the judicial system, even though there might be some psychological trauma associated with that course of action for the victim. The need to encourage the individual victim to remain in the system even at some psychological risk to herself was in order to bring about change and to restructure the judicial system for *future* victims, so that their ordeal would be minimized. But professional social workers began to argue for the individual client only and her resultant psychological crises. This case advocacy began to question the wisdom of using one client (as a cause) for the potential benefit of others. Class advocacy was being viewed as detrimental to the individual client. The primary responsibility of the social worker was to the client at hand (even at the expense of the many hiding in the bush!). The question became, is it the responsibility of social workers, particularly clinical social workers, to advocate for the improvement of the judicial system for all potential clients? What if that action seems to be in conflict with the self-determination of an individual client? Many social workers began resisting the more macro level change strategies and preferred to return their focus of concern solely to their client's intrapsychic material. Class (or cause) advocacy such as rape prevention classes, public education, and legal and judicial reform activities were given up in favor of the more direct clinical activities that presumably more directly met client needs. In several rape crisis programs, such class advocacy activities have now been completely replaced in favor of long-term followup with clients and their families. The "professionalization" of the rape center movement has resulted in a narrowing of focus—a "medicalizing" and "psychologizing" of the problem—a move away from the social/structural definition of the problem. Rape is again being seen as a problem that an individual victim needs help with to assist her adjustment to her trauma, *not* as a social problem within the context of societal violence, male aggression, and learned, dysfunctional sex role behaviors.

Clearly, advocacy models have changed over the last two decades. Even though the term was never well defined, its symbolic content has narrowed and now much more restrained and restricted models are being proffered. The role of the client/consumer has also changed. The next chapter examines how these changes in advocacy approaches have also influenced the rights of citizens. Roles, responsibilities and opportunities for citizens to plan for and participate in programs that affect their lives have slowly eroded over the last two decades. All citizens have been affected by these changes—but the poor, disabled and the seriously mentally ill perhaps have been affected the most.

Privatizing the Public Mandates

HISTORICAL SHIFTS OF RIGHTS

Advocacy, defined here as activities on behalf of others, was practiced by civil rights activists, community activists, students, and others in the mid-1960s. At that time, dramatic social changes were being brought about by the civil rights movement and the resultant civil rights legislation that outlawed discrimination on the basis of ethnicity, race, and sex. There was an emerging consensus that blacks and other minority groups had been systematically denied equal opportunities and the opportunity to participate fully in the benefits of society. Along with this belief came the concern that other citizens often excluded from active participation in decision making should be actively included in such decision making and begin to take control of the programs and policies that affect their communities and their lives. A belief emerged that they should become active in the political processes that influence their lives. Slowly these beliefs began to include not only the poor and the disenfranchised excluded by racial and sex bias, but also the disabled—such as the mentally retarded, the physically handicapped, and eventually, people with mental illnesses.

The nonviolent tactics of civil rights activists that had been successful in bringing about the passage of the 1964 Civil Rights Act were being modeled by students at universities, antiwar demonstrators, and others interested in using citizen power to dramatize their plight and bring about change. Saul Alinksy, a well known social activist who organized low-income communities in Chicago, taught through action that when disciplined and organized, even disenfranchised poor people could become powerful and bring about change in their communities (Alinsky, 1971). The federal government itself became active in forging coalitions among community action groups, social scientists, and politicians that resulted in an infusion of federal dollars for social experimentation in local communities. An optimism emerged that such coalitions could solve major social ills such as juvenile delinquency (the Grey Area Projects); school failures (the Elementary and Secondary Education Act of 1965); even poverty (the Economic Opportunity Act of 1964). After the death of President Kennedy, President Johnson, a master politician, built on the emerging consensus for social reform and waged a War on Poverty.

In 1964, the Economic Opportunity Act (EOA) was passed with a preamble that stated that the legislation was designed "to eliminate the paradox of poverty in the midst of plenty." An analysis of the actual Great Society programs show that they did not intend to change the social systems that affected the poor, but rather only change the way in which the poor participated in the existing system (Miringoff and Opdycke, 1986). Although many new program ideas were developed, funded, and implemented during the era of the Great Society, the programs that affected the truly poor remained mostly unchanged. Little real progress was obvious and the new initiatives began to be phased out, along with domestic funding cuts. Changes did take place in the *structure* of services. These changes still influence the role of the consumer, the advocate, and the federal government.

THE FEDERAL INITIATIVES

The federal government began experimenting with taking charge of creating programs and sometimes even becoming the service provider. It also began establishing funding opportunities and supporting programs directly to bring about change in the delivery of social services. An interesting twist that belied a federal centralist position permeated these legislative initiatives. Most clearly stated in the Community Action Program legislation of 1964, but woven throughout the entire EOA, was the stated willingness of the federal government to bypass established state and local governmental structures in order to create flexible, innovative, responsive programs and service delivery structures. In each title of the EOA, agreements were encouraged with "any federal, state, or local agency *or private organization*" [emphasis added]. The federal government was now reserving the right to delve past the traditional layers of state and county government to deal directly with community groups, organizations, and neighborhood agencies.

Current thinking assumed that the traditional structures from federal to local government were unresponsive and unable or unwilling to alter their modes of operation to include other styles of organization and implement different strategies for delivering social services. The enabling legislation that influenced most of the Johnson era initiatives and permeated its philosophy stated that the "recipients" of the services (and/or benefits) should be actively involved in the design and implementation of the program effort. Thus, now the federal government was offering new funds to be passed directly through state and local governments to community agencies. Furthermore, the federal government was encouraging advocacy for the disenfranchised by requiring participation of the consumers themselves in the design and implementation of service programs.

Title II of the EOA, which created the Community Action Program, explicitly stated that federal funds would be available to any *nonprofit group, public or private,* that developed programs towards the elimination of poverty, so long as the programs were "developed, constructed, and administered with the maximum feasible participation of residents of the areas and members of the groups served." This concept, often summarized as "maximum feasible participation," began an era of citizen participation and advocacy that still influences our political and policy making processes today. Every program funded by the federal government under its Community Action aegis, and later the Model Cities Program, Community Mental Health Centers Act, and others, mandated some form of citizen involvement in the planning, design, and implementation of how the dollars would be spent.

In the Community Mental Health Facilities Act (1963), rules and regulations specifically stated the percentage of "providers" and "consumers" who were eligible to serve on advisory and governing boards of community mental health centers using federal funds. Later refinements defined "primary" consumers as persons who actually were receiving mental health services. "Secondary" consumers were people who only secondarily benefited from the array of mental health services in their community. Primary and secondary providers also were distinguished as those service providers who received funds directly under the federal or state auspices and those persons who, while providing mental health services, were not direct beneficiaries of governmental dollars.

The War on Poverty historically may be seen as a series of program efforts that attempted to alter the way the federal government structured assistance to people and communities. It offered federal funds to a variety of new contractors for innovative service delivery schemes. Money was available for housing, health care, preschool education, child care, crime prevention programs, and a wide array of personal social services delivered at the community level with local participation and involvement in all stages of the process from planning through implementation to evaluation.

But contradictions abounded. The federal government was entering into areas where it had never ventured before. Programs such as Medicare, Medicaid, and Legal Aid were entirely new federal interventions. On the one hand, centralization was being attempted at least in terms of some federal involvement in social welfare issues. But there was also a parallel effort to decentralize and "pass through" federal dollars to small community-based organizations and interest groups, which marked a countervailing trend.

External historical events brought one phase of this experiment to a premature conclusion. The growing opposition to the war in Vietnam and the election of a Republican president in 1968 marked the beginning of a shift in the federal government's heavy influence in the design and funding of social welfare programs. Data show that from 1935 to 1980, American social policy, as seen in federal governmental decisions, flourished, with vastly expanded expenditures measured in constant dollars, in proportions of the GNP, and in per capita expenditures (Morris, 1987). From 1960 to 1982, the proportion of social welfare expenditures of the GNP, rose from 10.3 percent to 19.3 percent. Federal social insurance programs also rose as a proportion of all personal income from 6.8 percent to 13.9 percent. However, the programs designed for the most disadvantaged began to decline by 1982. Public aid and medical care decreased as a percentage of the GNP and programs such as child nutrition, the Office of Economic Opportunity, and Vocational Rehabilitation declined in absolute dollars as well.

THE TREND TO PRIVATIZE PUBLICLY MANDATED SOCIAL WELFARE

Perhaps an even more significant trend is the reliance on private or proprietary enterprises to take over conventional social welfare activities. A recent thrust in social policy has been to encourage public agencies to contract with proprietary ones for delivery of publicly funded services. Whereas nonprofit agencies had long been assumed to be the most appropriate alternative to the governmental provision of services, profit-oriented agencies are now being considered to be more efficient and less costly. Furthermore, the voluntary agencies are being described as wasteful and lacking in managerial skills.

By 1984, contracting out or direct reimbursement of proprietary agencies had become commonplace. Morris (1987:92) suggests that due to these changes, one of two outcomes is likely: Either the social service field will come to behave more like a business than a community service, or the community will divide responsibility between the better off, who will use proprietary services, and the less affluent, who use nonprofit or public services. In the field of mental illness, this division has already taken place. Services for people with the most serious and persistent mental illness are the responsibility of the public sector, whereas the "worried well" are happily being referred to the private provider, who is more interested and better trained to deal with such clients.

Confidence in the federal government's ability to perform social functions well or efficiently has declined dramatically, too. Republican pledges to reduce the authority of the federal government hit a responsive chord with the American public. The rising costs of welfare seemed to reach a saturation point as well as a limit of public acceptance. Furthermore, many of the government-run or government-designed programs have neither been able to demonstrate their effectiveness nor document success, thus increasing the disillusionment with the impact of applied social science as an effective social problem solver. Disillusionment with the role of "consumer as expert" and the role of the federal government as service delivery provider spread rapidly. Presidents Nixon, Ford, and Carter all took steps to dismantle the federal government's role in social welfare programming and moved actively towards decentralization, with the states gaining control of the funds and program priorities related to social welfare. In 1972, the State and Local Fiscal Assistance Act authorized $30.2 billion to states and localities based on a formula using population size, tax effort, tax collections, per capita income, and urbanization as criteria (Terrell, 1976). President Nixon boosted this idea of revenue sharing as a great catalyst for democracy, a way to return "power to the people" by shifting decision making from "out of touch" Washington bureaucrats to the grassroots citizens most aware and knowledgeable about their local circumstances and needs. Federal money under the revenue sharing system was relatively unrestricted and the responsibility for appropriate implementation fell squarely on the shoulders of the state and local governments. This shift away from specific or categorical funds, for which the government held the grantee accountable, was expected to improve program accountability, efficiency, and responsiveness.

Advocates of this revenue sharing approach assumed that decentralizing decisions and funds would increase the influence of local citizens and thus invigorate local politics. Supporters expected that this approach would increase community interest and involvement in the local policy making processes. Others warned that the geographic proximity of local citizens to their elected decision makers would not necessarily result in an increase in the political sensitivity of decision makers. They warned that non-earmarked funds would result in a reduced commitment to social welfare services generally since local units of government are typically more beholden to commercial interests and politically powerful elites and are generally unsympathetic to human services (Etzioni, 1973). Thus, while revenue sharing was not a specific piece of legislation, its approach dramatically altered the way social services were to be funded, delivered, administered, and evaluated.

SOME DISTURBING TRENDS

Several trends are now patently clear. Human service spending by the federal government has been cut drastically. The use of private agencies to deliver publicly funded services, through contracting out or purchase of service arrangements, has increased dramatically. The role of citizens as participants in planning, designing, implementing, monitoring, and evaluating programs has decreased substantially.

Public opinion is clearly in favor of less government and more passive government. Disillusionment with the federal government's ability to manage (let alone solve) intractable social problems has become a popular political theme over the last decade. American values of efficiency and self reliance have been translated into less government involvement and intervention. Now the political theme that results in voter approval calls for reversing the growth of governmental programs. They are now seen as too large, inefficient, and ineffective. Twenty years ago the rallying calls for action were for increased federal intervention, since the existing state and local programs were deemed as unsympathetic, unresponsive, and unpopular. Now the complaints are against the government's involvement and the calls are to support the entry of private enterprise on the social welfare scene.

President Reagan's 1980 campaign themes and a major thrust of his administration were to aggressively continue the efforts to decentralize and reduce the size and scope of federal intervention in the area of domestic programs. The goals of efficiency and effectiveness became the catchwords of the era, replacing the calls for responsiveness and sensitivity. A feeling that the taxpayers had done enough replaced the notion that more must be done to help others. Lower domestic spending, rigorous means testing (to insure that only the most needy received any benefits), and a strictly limited government role in social policy and programs became America's popular, "traditional" values. A focus on rugged individualism, self-reliance, and a basic distrust for a large governmental role in problem solving were the politically popular phrases of the day.

The Omnibus Budget Reconciliation Act of 1981 not only substantially cut federal funding for many social welfare programs, it dramatically expanded the revenue sharing principle that returned the decision making processes concerning social services to the states.

Hundreds of existing federal grants for a wide range of purposes were consolidated into a few "block" grants, leaving the states with the authority and responsibility to fund, cut, or revise any programs they wished. The federal government encouraged the states to establish their own goals and required little from them in terms of planning, monitoring, or service assurances.

It was expected that the shift of decision making from a centralized governmental focus in Washington, D. C., to fifty separate governors and fifty separate legislatures would provide a competitive stimulus to each state to provide cost effective, high-quality services that were responsive to the specific needs of the residents of each state. However, the coordination costs, monitoring expenses, and contracting arrangements led to a complicated array of services of questionable benefit and effectiveness. The *providers* of services benefited from this locally based decision making and the new infusion of purchase of service arrangements. For the *client*, on the other hand, finding an appropriate service and being able to afford it was not an easy task. Now there were hundreds of thousands of providers with little organizational relationship to those administering their funds. Little overall planning and design of services took place and the social service "system" became even more fragmented than before, with little effort made to coordinate the system. The resultant decentralized network of service providers was difficult to evaluate and almost impossible to monitor.

Response to these problems were primarily to call for more coordination of the services. Creating more coordinating councils, umbrella agencies, more planning services, or as Miringoff (1986) once suggested, "an agency for coordinating coordinating agencies," was unlikely to bring about any noticeable improvement. A major problem in the attempt to coordinate such a disparate array of service providers was that such efforts lacked the ability to control or even alter the system they were attempting to coordinate. Often these coordinating attempts had extremely broad goals but extremely limited powers. While reducing the costs of coordination would have greatly increased the efficiency of these (or any) efforts, little was done to achieve this.

STRATEGIES FOR IMPROVED COORDINATION AND MORE CENTRALIZED AUTHORITY

While it seemed to be a well-accepted principle that decentralization and local autonomy improves efficiency, it is an empirical question whether a complex institution such as the social welfare system can function effectively with a highly decentralized structure. Not only are there issues of "real" coordination (monitoring contracts, assessing accessibility, quality of care, responsiveness to needs), but there is also the issue (perhaps unique to social welfare) of attracting and maintaining public support. The shift toward decentralized public social services, with an emphasis on purchase of service contracts and professional competition, results in the (perhaps) unintended consequence of defining many of the social problems in individualistic terms. For example, poverty during the War on Poverty effort was conceptualized as a community-based problem. This definition resulted in an array of rehabilitative and reconstructive strategies founded on a systemic analysis of unemployment compounded with racism that limited the opportunities for large groups of disenfranchised people. The more recent privatizing models of social welfare lack this broader vision and have returned to a case-by-case (or family-by-family) analysis of poverty that stresses individual deficiencies, personal lacks, and defects. Private practice social workers now frequently mimic the role of private psychologists who search only within the individual and suggest individualistic change. The individual in the context of the environment has been redefined in recent social work practice to mean, "How does a practitioner reshape and mold the individual to better resonate with the dominant system?" Previously, professional social workers asked, "What elements of the community, institutions, and political structures support individuals and maximize their self-actualization?" and which ones don't? This type of analysis is sorely missing in today's social work training, ideology and resultant practice.

But perhaps even more important is the fact that this type of analysis is sorely missing in today's public policy and political debates. Specialized, technically correct, efficient, and effective interventions by highly trained professionals who are accountable primarily to their professional code of ethics and behavioral standards reduce the community's ability to truly assess its social problems and its social progress. The cost of doing social welfare "business" now is assessed by the professional's satisfaction with the contract being offered by the funding source. Rarely is a consumer/client/recipient voice heard (or even requested) to assess the service provided or the quality of the "goods" received. This is a dramatic shift from the consumer involvement movement so active in the 1960s. Issues such as coordination (along with accountability, efficiency, etc.) were being discussed as crucial goals during the 1980s, with social workers particularly being asked to demonstrate their ability to prove their "impact bang for the buck." As the public system of social welfare became a private system of professionals selling their wares, the focus shifted subtly towards "resistant clients of the underclass," and away from the systemic causes or even the professionals' ability to bring about change successfully. Blaming the victim avoids any look at a failure in the structure of the service delivery system to apply appropriate interventions.

Gilbert's *Capitalism and the Welfare State* (1983) suggests that the term "welfare capitalism" may be understood as the insinuation of the profit motive onto the previously not-for-profit public welfare activities of the government. And whereas before the 1960s, there were clear distinctions between the "public" and "private" sectors of the welfare system, now such distinctions are rare. Purchase of service contracting with public money funding private agencies for the delivery of human services has become big business. Billions are paid annually by state and local governments to private agencies.

The contracting-out process (or purchase of service contract) has several phases. The process begins with a community analysis and assessment of needs (Kettner and Martin, 1985). The volume and types of services needed are identified and available resources are inventoried. Implications for citizen participation and involvement here are obvious. If there is any remaining notion that the consumers/clients themselves have a role in identifying the form and structure of the service to insure relevance and appropriateness, then this is the time for their input. Citizen/consumer input should logically be requested to insure that such services will be appropriate and that a relevant service strategy will be offered to the community. Terrell (1976) found that in California in the early years of the revenue sharing process, "citizens" had been actively involved in initiating governmental social revenue sharing commitments, competing for funds, structuring requests for proposals, evaluating proposals, and in some situations monitoring and evaluating the contracts (Terrell:105). This form of involvement typically included testifying at public hearings, lobbying, and coalition forming among community organizations and advisory groups. Terrell raised a concern about who actually would be the consumers who participated in the decisions related to service delivery. It became clear rather quickly that citizen participation merely became a euphemism for "agency" participation. What has become of the voice for the unrepresented and underrepresented minorities? Who speaks for those not aligned with popular causes or agency interests? The contracting out to private agencies for public services has changed the voice of advocacy in that consumer/citizen power has progressively become agency power. Power for the social agency—or perhaps power for the professional—has replaced the cry for power for the people. Advocates for the disabled, the disenfranchised, and the unpopular have become synonymous with professional advocates working to increase their agency's resources. Now private practitioners themselves compete for contracts to provide publicly mandated social services. Their reference group is frequently the contracting source, not the client they are to serve.

GRANTS VERSUS CONTRACTS

A seemingly small and subtle administrative distinction—that between a purchase of service contract and a grant to a private agency—has brought about significant changes in social service delivery and the role of advocates. When a government agency provides funding to a private social welfare agency for the purpose of providing care or services to clients, a contract relationship is deemed to exist. However, when a government agency provides funding to a private social agency to assist it in discharging the private agency's own functioning, a grant is said to exist (Kettner and Martin, 1985). Under a contract arrangement, the recipients/clients/consumers are public agency clients, while under the grant the recipients are considered to be the clients of the private agency. The amount and type of information the government can expect to receive from a private agency about its clientele varies as the relationship between the funding agency and the service agency changes. The amount of citizen involvement and consumer evaluation in the process also changes depending on the arrangement between the public and private sectors. The data available to an advocacy organization wishing to learn about the type and quality of services being provided by the state through a private organization has been severely restricted through this private enterprise model. Even the granting agency itself has an extremely difficult time keeping track of its contracts and how and where the money is being spent.

The request for proposal (RFP) stage of the purchase-of-service (POS) system has influenced the role of consumer input. A request-for-proposal process is initiated after a needs assessment in the community has been completed. The RFP is a document describing a needed service and requesting that providers come forth with proposals detailing a service delivery strategy and the expected costs necessary to provide that service. When proposals are received, they are evaluated and the most cost effective provider that can provide the needed services presumably is awarded the contract. It is presumed that having multiple, competing contractors strengthens the government contracting agency's hand in ensuring accountability, and that the competition between providers and agencies will cut costs. The involvement of citizens into the decision making process at this stage varies state by state. Provider councils have been formed in some states to review the RFPs, which certainly brings into question the role and influence of the consumers.

Kettner and Martin (1985) reviewed the issues of monitoring the purchase of service contracts. In their conclusion they list sixteen features of a well designed monitoring system. They emphasize the necessity of clearly worded POS rationales, timely monitoring by knowledgeable monitors, and the need for a professional collaborative relationship between the monitors and the contracts, among others. However, they never once suggest that the recipients of the services be included in the evaluation of the services provided. Cursory monitoring of contract compliance may result in only the quantitative and most easily measurable items being assessed. For example, if a contract to provide mental health services is let to a private agency, would the number of clients visiting the agency be a measure of success? Or would the number of clients not visiting the program and living independently be a better measure of success (albeit more difficult to document)? How would a contract that attempts to foster independent living be monitored? Seeing only a few clients might be a success or it might be evidence of neglect. Establishing a well designed evaluation study to determine the results of the agency's practice interventions is extremely costly.

Richter and Ozawa (1983) raise another question related to the impact of federal funds on a private agency's ability to be politically active while advocating for social action. It is hypothesized that as the level of governmental funding increases in proportion to the private agency's total budget, the agency will become less involved and less active in criticizing the service delivery system that feeds them. Who will speak out for clients if even the voluntary, not-for-profit private agencies are being funded by public funds—particularly if those funds increasingly support a larger and larger proportion of the future funds of these agencies?

THE CHANGING ROLE OF PROFESSIONAL SOCIAL WORK

The funding levels for social services have been cut back and the structure of the service delivery system has changed significantly. How have these changes affected professional social work? How have these changes affected social work and their relationships to their clients?

The following table outlines this change over time:

Role of S. W.	Focus of Concern	Focus of Activity
Advocate	Client	Change System Obtain Resources Increase Services
Enabler	Client	Education Mobilization Facilitation
Empowerer	Client	Skill Building Gain Political Power Acquire Political Rights
Contractee/POS	Agency/Self	Lobbying Grant Writing Resource Development

As the shift from federal to state funds has taken place, so has the need of professional social work to alter its relationship to its clients. From a stance of "advocating for others," "championing the cause of others," social work is now becoming skilled in advocating for the social service agencies that hire them. And while these activities indirectly assist clients who are served by these agencies, the development of corporate boards of directors in place of volunteer boards of directors, fund development coordinators in place of volunteer coordinators, and CEOs in place of executive directors has certainly changed the thrust and feeling of the work of social agencies and raises some questions about the workers' relationships to their clients.

What has happened to the role of the citizen/client/consumer as the structure and funding of social service agencies changes?

The following table outlines this change:

Changing Role of Citizen Participation	
Role of Social Worker	Focus of Concern
Advocate	Client Self-Determination
Enabler	Client Self-Betterment
Empowerer	Client Influence
Contractee/POS Recipient	Client as Unit of Service

As this table shows, the role of the social worker and the role of the citizen as participant in service delivery systems have changed. The focus of advocacy has shifted and become more complex and more professionalized. The following chapter will describe these changes, using advocacy efforts on behalf of persons with serious and persistent mental illnesses as examples.

The Advocacy Organizations

Efforts to help people with emotional disorders, behavioral problems, and mental illnesses have gone on for centuries. And while it is estimated that almost 15 percent of the population in the United States will need the assistance of a mental health expert during their lifetimes, definitional problems regarding mental health and mental illness still abound. Mental health is not a precise term, but rather an intuitively agreed upon idea that may vary in time and across cultures. At one extreme, mental illness (see Scheff, 1966) has been conceptualized as no more than an agreed upon set of behaviors that have been defined as deviant. But to a person hearing voices and feeling that he or she is losing control of their mind and behavior, mental illness is a very real disease.

Mental illness may be considered as a medical, psychological, physiological, or social phenomenon. Thus, mental illness, which is more than the absence of mental health, also may have many different causal theories and suppositions as to its etiology, prevalence, duration, and cure.

So what is mental illness? When does a person become an appropriate target for intervention? What types of services are appropriate? Who should provide them? Where should the services be provided? Who should pay for them? Who is responsible for the provision of the services? Should the services be voluntary? How one answers these questions, among others, is tied to one's perspective of mental health and mental illness. Different ideological perspectives impinge on the emerging scientific approaches and result in different people having quite different definitions of mental illness, causal theories, priority intervention programs, needed policies, and system designs. Different historical eras have approached mental illness differently and today there still remains a wide range of concepts and practices operating concurrently for helping the mentally ill.

Jeger and Slotnick (1982:2–6) suggest that there are five major models of psychopathology that are currently guiding mental health practice. These models also influence the laws, policies, and treatment approaches that surround mental health issues today. It is the contention of this author that until the major elements of these different models are joined into a congruent model of action, the services and policies for mentally ill persons will remain fragmented, disjointed, and woefully inadequate. Until the advocacy organizations join together in their efforts and form a united front with similar perspectives, the interorganizational differences will divide them and only serve to keep mentally ill people unserved and underserved.

FIVE CONTEMPORARY VIEWS OF MENTAL HEALTH PRACTICE

Jeger and Slotnick (1982) name the five major models of psychopathology that are guiding current mental health practice as follows: (1) biological/medical, (2) psychodynamic/intrapsychic, (3) behavioral/learning, (4) humanistic, and (5) social/sociocultural. These models in turn have professional mental health experts aligned with them and there are major advocacy groups also following these different perspectives.

The Medical Model

The biological/medical model is the oldest and perhaps still the most authoritative model in practice. This model views mental health problems as rooted in the physiology of the person. This might include disorders or "diseases" of the brain, problems with the functioning of the central nervous system, biochemical and biophysical disturbances, and/or genetic anomalies (Kety et al., 1968; DSM III, 1980; Cloninger et al., 1975). This perspective sees mental illness as closely aligned with other physical illnesses, although the manifestation of the disease is in the brain and thus affects thinking and behavior (Torrey, 1986). The focus of this perspective is on research to find the part of the brain that is diseased or the gene that is the carrier of the abnormality. Treatment protocols focus primarily on medication and drug management. Supporters of this approach see the hospital as the main locus for treatment, with psychiatrists as the logical leaders of any treatment team.

The Psychodynamic Approach

The psychodynamic model of mental illness was developed by Dr. Sigmund Freud. Rather than examining the person for a physiologically based disorder, this approach looks for problems within the person's psychological structure and examines psychological determinants, stresses, conflicts, and strengths. Early childhood developmental stages are explored and believed to be determinants of later personality structuring (Richmond, 1917; Freud, 1914; Fromme-Reichman, 1950). The unconscious is a crucial element of the psychodynamic approach and therapists from this school work with clients to develop insight into one's own functioning. This model is parallel to the medical model in that it sees mental illness as a symptom of some underlying cause and treats patients through diagnosis to cure. A complex array of intervention techniques have been designed based on the rich theory of personality developed by Freud.

The profession of social work particularly has clung to this model and it has been a major influence among its practitioners. Four basic assumptions guide this perspective: Each individual has a unique personality structure that includes conflicting forces yet remains relatively stable over time; there are myriad unconscious elements that influence an individual's behavior; relationships and experiences with significant others during early childhood shape one's later responses and relationships; and current and future social functioning can be improved through gaining insight into the causes and effects of one's perceptions (Watkins, 1983).

The focus of treatment is usually one-to-one psychotherapy with attempts to alter the abnormal personality through the development of insight into the causes of the problems. The medical model is still the basic framework utilized since the mental illness is seen as a symptom of some underlying cause, which the patient must fully confront, understand, and master to become well. Early psychoanalytic training required that a therapist complete a medical degree before becoming a fully trained psychoanalyst. These therapists use techniques such as dream interpretation, free association, and insight development exercises to assist their patients. Today, psychiatrists still dominate the field of therapists using the psychodynamic approach, but other professionals such as clinical psychologists, social workers, and psychiatric nurses also use these methods. The locus of this care is most frequently outpatient clinics, although this form of treatment is often used in conjunction with medication protocols.

The Behaviorist Approach

The behavioral model of mental health practice views the problem of mental disorders as learned behaviors. Behaviorism attends to the observable acts in social interaction. Rather than exploring unconscious motivations, early life experiences, and feelings, the focus of this approach is on what specific actions the client is concerned about and the factors in the client's social environment that precede, accompany, and follow these behaviors. This perspective contends that maladaptive behaviors evidenced have been learned and thus acquired from the environment through reinforcements and lack of reinforcements. According to this perspective, people whom others define as mentally ill have had faulty learning and should not be considered sick. Rather, this approach sees maladaptive behavior as a failing in the learning processes. It contends that through classical conditioning, modeling, and cognitive learning or restructuring, "normal" behaviors can be acquired (see Skinner, 1938; Ullmann and Krasner, 1975; Leitenberg, 1976; Thomas, 1977).

The treatment protocols of behaviorists are based mainly on operant conditioning techniques (Ayllon and Azrin, 1968), modeling (Bandura, 1977), and cognitive learning principles (Mahoney, 1977). All of these approaches assume that a client will unlearn maladaptive behaviors and learn new and adaptive responses. Training programs in developing positive self-change have been widely evaluated and found to be extremely successful, particularly when clearly defined problems (such as phobias, certain types of depressions, social skills deficiencies, etc.) can be identified and are selected for change.

While the behavioral approach is an alternative to the medically based disease model, the orientation and intervention structures remain quite parallel. Most behaviorist interventions are conducted by professionally trained psychologists, who offer "therapy" or "treatment" in mental health clinics or private offices in one-to-one settings or sometimes small group environments. The responsibility for the behavioral change of the client, however, is put on the shoulders of the client. Individualistically designed reinforcement schedules are drawn up by the client and carefully tailored intervention strategies are organized based on the client's input.

Humanistic Approaches

The humanistic model, most aligned with Carl Rogers (Rogers, 1970; Perls, 1969), sees psychological distress as a form of "alienation from oneself." Problems are viewed in terms of the gap between the ideal self and the real self. Intervention techniques, often done in group encounters or one-to-one counseling, focus on teaching the client to accept him or herself with positive regard. This helps the client feel better and, through self-actualization, become more able to cope with life's stresses and to achieve his or her objectives in life. Treatment protocols involve nondirective therapy that provides an environment in which a client may explore feelings in an effort to increase acceptance. The therapist structures an environment of acceptance, warmth, and empathy for the client that helps the client develop personal authenticity and strength.

This approach is now widely practiced by psychologists and social workers, as well as self-taught counselors who may not have had formal training in the therapeutic techniques. The locus of care is usually not within traditional mental health clinics, but may be offered in churches; through private, not-for-profit agencies; or by profit-making therapists and centers. The clients best served through this technique are those looking for "personal growth" and to develop their human potential. It is not a model that has been successfully implemented with the seriously mentally ill.

The Sociocultural Viewpoint

The sociocultural model of mental illness sees the causes of the problem (and thus, the strategies for change) within the social structural arrangements of society rather than within the individual. Social problems such as poor housing conditions, racism, and poverty are seen as the underlying causes of individual stress that adversely affect a person's functioning and can bring about severe mental disabilities. Interventions seek to alleviate these social problems and change the social and environmental stressors of which a person is a part. This view thus looks at the external environment as the cause of stress rather than looking within the individual. But whereas the behaviorist view looks at immediate, clearly definable, and manipulative stressors, the sociocultural model looks at the macroenvironmental stressors and sees political and social change as necessary to decrease mental illnesses. Advocates of this approach often are political activists and social change agents who see change as necessary to improve society for the masses, not only those suffering from mental distress. Political change, rather than individualistic change, is the focus of the supporters of this approach (Szasz, 1961; Scheff, 1966; Brenner, 1973; Szasz, 1971).

A Composite Model

Jerger and Slotnick (1982) have conceptualized a composite model called the behavioral-ecological approach. This model focuses both on the individual behavior of a client as well as on the stressors in the environment and then examines the interactions and transactions between them. An ecological perspective that includes an examination of communities, environments, and social systems is combined with the behavioral approaches derived from psychology. This perspective assumes that there is a reciprocal influence between people and their environments and that appropriate interventions would include activities on both levels—individual and community. Individual level help is reconceptualized as "training for competence." People may need to be taught to gain access to environmental resources and design their own environments in accordance with their own goals.

The original idea of the Community Mental Health Center Act of 1963 was to blend these divergent perspectives into a coherent practice. But moving away from the dominant medical model has been extremely difficult and very slow; it has met with tremendous resistance from doctors and consumers alike.

THE PERSEVERANCE OF THE MEDICAL MODEL

Recently, however, the medical model has begun to be challenged, particularly in the face of the national deinstitutionalization policies. Researchers have clearly documented the ineffectiveness of long-term hospital stays as a treatment for mental illness (Stein and Test, 1985). The introduction of antipsychotic medications has significantly altered the form and structure of the delivery of mental health services. Almost all of the research in the last decade has demonstrated the effectiveness of community-based treatment programs, when coupled with adequate support systems (Stein and Test, 1978; Test and Stein, 1978; Bachrach, 1984). Yet the dichotomy—hospital versus community-based treatment—is still being played out not only in policy debates, but among mental health professionals, consumer groups, advocates, and legislators.

THE ADVOCATES' DEBATE

Advocates of the medical model continue to see the hospital as a major locus of care for mentally ill persons. They favor laws and administrative policies that support easy access to hospitalization and medication even if it is against a client's will. Advocates of other approaches, however, have been actively supporting legislative and administrative changes aimed at protecting the rights of mentally ill people. Legislative changes beginning in the early 1960s began altering the mental health professional's authority to treat and commit to mental institutions patients who do not want such treatment. Recognition that a person involuntarily committed to a state institution due to a mental illness loses many of his or her citizenship rights such as the right to vote, receive mail, or work, became the grounds for a spate of legal actions and civil rights cases taken on behalf of the institutionalized mentally ill. Court cases defining such terms as "mentally ill," "dangerousness," and "treatment in the least restrictive (or most therapeutic) environment" began to redefine the scope and limits of mental health practice. The courts also began to define a person's right to treatment as well as the right to refuse treatment (Miller, 1987).

THE HISTORICAL ROLE OF ADVOCATES: FROM ASYLUMS TO THE STREETS AGAIN

Reformers such as Dorothea Dix in the mid-nineteenth century began crusades to provide asylums for the mentally disordered. These asylums were to be humane facilities for the mentally disabled, who frequently were left to wander and beg in the streets or were put into prisons mixed with criminals. At this time, there was little known about mental illness and thus little effective treatment or services were provided. Dorothea Dix's efforts to protect mentally ill persons were seen as a humanistic crusade designed to protect people who could not protect themselves. Her tireless teaching and advocacy changed the notions of defining mentally ill persons as "possessed with demons" to people in need of asylum (Grob, 1983). When these new asylums were first built, entry was easily accomplished and the admission procedures were largely informal. A physician, friend, or even a relative could merely apply to a hospital superintendent to admit a person they considered mentally ill. There was no legal or judicial procedure necessary to commit a person to a mental institution.

But as the asylums filled up with chronic patients whose conditions merely worsened, the institutions themselves worsened and care deteriorated. Another reform movement developed to protect the rights of those already committed as well as to call for the development of procedures to protect against wrongful commitments (Rothman, 1980). Courts throughout the nation began to hear cases about the infringement of the rights of the mentally ill incarcerated in state mental institutions. The courts began to make distinctions among the categories of the mentally ill, the poor, and the criminal offender. Later criteria were developed under which one could justify incarceration. However, the standards for mentally ill persons were being expressed in medical language, and psychiatrists remained the primary "experts" in defining the category of mental illness. Physicians, usually psychiatrists, were allowed to set the standards for the definitions of mental illness as well as the treatment protocols required.

If a person was characterized by a doctor as "being mentally ill and in need of treatment," this usually sufficed as grounds for treatment; even treatment including involuntary hospitalization. But the reliability of a physician's diagnosis began to be challenged as the basis for depriving people of their liberty. Ennis and Litwak's research (1974) convincingly demonstrated that psychiatrists diagnosing the same patient will agree on the same diagnosis less than 50 percent of the time. They concluded that such a poor level of agreement could not be the criterion used to deprive persons of their liberty. Schizophrenia particularly has been a disease most frequently misdiagnosed and overdiagnosed, and yet it remains the basis for most of the involuntary commitments in the United States.

CIVIL RIGHTS REFORMS AND THE ASSAULT ON THE STATE INSTITUTIONS

During the civil rights movements of the 1970s, the pressure to apply procedural protections from the criminal justice system to civil commitments of mentally ill persons grew. Merely being diagnosed as mentally ill by a physician was now being questioned as sufficient grounds for incarceration. Several states introduced a clause in their civil commitment laws that stated that persons must be both mentally ill *and* a danger to themselves or others before an *ex-parte* order to commit would be granted.

In 1972, a federal district court in Wisconsin held in *Lessard v. Schmidt* that evidence of imminent danger to self or others was constitutionally necessary for involuntary commitment to a mental institution. The court also reaffirmed that a mentally ill person must be granted the same procedural protections of due process found in *re*: Gault during a commitment hearing. (In *re*: Gault, 387 U.S. 1 [1967], the Supreme Court found that juveniles facing the potential loss of liberty, and the stigma associated with being incarcerated, required the same due process protections, including representation by counsel, as were provided to adult criminal defendants.) The U. S. Supreme Court to date has not clearly decided if dangerousness is a constitutional necessity for civil commitment. However, mentally ill persons are now assured the right to treatment if institutionalized and must not be involuntarily institutionalized without due process. The various states continue to legislate different laws regarding the definitions of mental illness and continue to create their own civil commitment statutes.

CIVIL COMMITMENT LAWS IN THE DEINSTITUTIONALIZATION ERA

An interesting shift of concern has again taken place. Now there is a "reform" effort underway that contends that mentally ill persons are being neglected and left to care for themselves, often on the streets. The new phenomenon of the homeless has among its ranks people who previously would have been living in state mental institutions. Due to the aggressive deinstitutionalization policies of most states and the legal protections against involuntarily committing a mentally ill person to a state hospital, it has become extremely difficult to commit a person without evidence of an act of dangerousness to oneself or another person. Many advocate groups, most notably the National Alliance for the Mentally Ill, have argued that it is now too difficult to involuntarily admit a person to a mental hospital until it is too late. They contend that waiting until there is an act of violence is inhumane and have become active advocates for legislative reforms that would ease commitment criteria.

In the late 1970s a number of states began the process of relaxing their commitment criteria by introducing the category of "grave disability." This term has been defined in most states as the inability to provide for one's basic needs of food, clothing, and shelter. It is being used as an alternative to the "dangerousness to oneself" standard, which in many states required that there be an overt act of violence as evidence that a person was a danger to him or herself. The gravely disabled standard has been criticized as unconstitutionally vague by attorneys and insulting by consumer groups, but to date it has been upheld by the district courts and is now the law in many states.

Language such as "obviously ill" also has been introduced in some states as grounds for civil commitment and to date has not been constitutionally challenged. Hawaii and North Carolina have adopted laws permitting lesser standards to be used to mandate outpatient psychiatric treatment. These changes have occurred primarily due to the activity of mental health professionals and family members of mentally ill persons. These groups believe that in the post-deinstitutional era, it has become almost impossible to institutionalize a person needing mental health care unless that person is willing to enter the institution voluntarily. Some feel that many mentally ill persons are being neglected and are not receiving the mental health treatment that they desperately need. These newer laws that ease admission standards, for a variety of reasons, have rarely been used and it is unclear if they have helped or hindered the mentally ill. Patients' rights advocates, however, have noted with alarm the softening of civil commitment standards and have decried the return to clinically based standards for commitment purposes. They see a dangerous tautology in a procedure that permits the definition of mental illness to be "a condition requiring treatment." And they fear any clinical usurping of judicial authority.

CONVERGING TRENDS: MENTALLY ILL PEOPLE ARE BEING NOTICED AGAIN

In the United States, several trends have converged recently to once again draw attention to the plight of the seriously and persistently mentally ill. During the 1960s, factual accounts of blatant cruelty within isolated state mental institutions so outraged the public that an examination of the rights of patients began anew. Public interest attorneys, often funded by Legal Aid and the Public Defender offices, began to confront the authority of the psychiatrist and state hospital's institutional staff. A thorough examination of the rights of the institutionalized in public facilities took place. The civil rights protections being granted to the poor, ethnic minorities, and other handicapped groups were beginning to be extended to people committed to public instititutions such as jails, prisons, juvenile facilities, and mental institutions.

THE UNIQUE DILEMMA OF HELPING THE MENTALLY ILL

Protecting the rights of psychiatric patients has always been seen as particularly difficult since the illness itself makes the client not fully rational at times and thus problematic to help. The advocacy efforts of people working on behalf of mentally ill persons frequently conflict, owing largely to the perspective on mental illness the particular advocacy group holds. The advocacy stance of the psychiatric/mental health professional differs substantially from that of the attorney. (The positions of advocacy organizations, civil rights groups, patient groups, and family members will be discussed later.) There is a fundamental disagreement between attorneys and mental health professionals in the orientation to the services delivered to mentally ill persons.

THE ADVOCATES: THE ATTORNEY VERSUS THE MENTAL HEALTH PROFESSIONAL

The operating style of the attorney is to determine what the client wants. The very term "client" as opposed to "patient" highlights a difference in perspective. The attorney provides the client with information and may suggest a few beneficial strategies to the client, but the basic perspective of the attorney is to work *for* the client and see his/her wishes met. The mental health professional, on the other hand, is trained to diagnose a patient and, after a thorough assessment, prescribe what is best for the patient. The patient is expected to comply with the professional's judgment and at times the professional may even interpret a patient's resistance to accept what the professional offers as a manifestation of the illness. The mental health professional often must act in ways the client disagrees with; these activities are validated (at least within the profession) as being in the best interest of the client. Attorneys often complain that a client's rights are too easily sacrificed by the mental health professional's efforts to do what is clinically best for mentally ill persons.

A particularly complex dilemma is the fact that the treatment and services offered to mentally ill persons are frequently of limited effectiveness. Most attorneys are reluctant to deprive a person of his or her liberty by means of a civil commitment if commitment will be to an institution in which treatment effectiveness is as yet unproven. This is often of particular concern to the attorney when the patient has previously been in such an institution and is unwilling to comply with the mental health professional's recommendations for additional or continued treatment. Whether such a person's assessment is irrational or completely sane may itself be the nub of the disagreement between the attorney's position for a client and the mental health professional's concern for a patient.

ADVOCACY ON BEHALF OF THE MENTALLY ILL

Advocacy has been defined by Lourie (1975) as "a device for increasing pressures against the social structure to achieve social equity and justice." With regard to mentally ill persons, however, the activities associated with promoting a cause or pleading a case on behalf of another are extremely broad and at times in conflict with one another.

For example, advocacy has been used as a synonym for case management or even direct psychotherapy. An interdisciplinary mental health team at a community mental health center that is responsible for delivering an array of treatment services for a client is often called a client/advocacy team. This service advocacy team is usually oriented to individual clients on a case by case basis and is concerned with providing appropriate available services. While such advocates may indeed work on behalf of clients and improve their service package, they are severely restricted in their ability to change the system since they are a part of it. Also they have little power or resources to develop additional or different service systems. Thus they "advocate" for clients by bringing them the status quo. (And while at times this may be more than clients have been receiving before, it is not an activist stance to improving the services for the mentally ill.)

Advocacy on behalf of clients as a class or group has been called class advocacy, or more recently, policy advocacy. This form of advocacy is focused on changing administrative policies, legislative statutes, and programmatic decisions that impinge on the lives of the mentally ill. Interestingly, this type of advocacy is most often done by organizations not directly involved with the delivery of services. For example, mental health associations, protection and advocacy organizations, and self-help organizations have been the most successful in bringing about policy and administrative changes on behalf of the mentally ill. The mental health professionals themselves and their professional organizations have a self-interest in the individualistic clinical implications of policy decisions and often are less interested, able, or willing to advocate for macro-level change.

Lourie (1975) also suggests that there is a distinction between legal advocacy and operational advocacy. Legal advocacy, such as the activities of the Mental Health Law Project in Washington, D. C., use the law to achieve social purposes and redress current social wrongs. Attorneys take individual and class action cases into court in an effort to win additional rights or more often to insure the implementation, enforcement, and expansion of rights that psychiatric patients have already won in some other jurisdiction. Operational advocacy, on the other hand, is concerned with the human service delivery system. A client may have the right to receive a service, but the appropriate service that is either not available or not accessible to the client is a right denied. Operational advocacy seeks to insure that the necessary and appropriate services are provided to the consumers in need of them.

A classic example of this dilemma is the community-based program for the seriously mentally ill. Research has consistently demonstrated that these clients do best when placed in community-based programs with professional backup services, counseling, and access to crisis intervention. However, many states have not developed community-based programs and instead let the state hospital serve as the main facility of choice when a crisis occurs with a mentally ill person. Legal, policy, and operational advocates contend that the funding emphasis must shift away from state hospitals towards community programs. Service advocates, however, who perhaps agree in principle, frequently fight for increased funding of the state hospital, because the community programs do not exist and they must have treatment facilities for the mentally ill person who today is on their caseload.

Family members of mentally ill people have become active allies of the service advocates since their focus is the person at hand in need of immediate services and a secure place to live. Many have argued that the failures of the deinstitutionalization movement were the failures of the legal and policy advocates who ignored the ramifications of their actions. Successful in increasing the civil rights of mentally ill patients in hospitals, these advocates failed miserably in designing and developing the community-based services that these patients would need when they were released from the hospitals. Some have said that mentally ill persons in America now "die in the streets with their rights on."

The challenge for the coming decade for all those concerned about mental illness will be to organize mental health services in a manner that protects both civil and clinical rights. Advocacy is a technique commonly used by mental health practitioners to intervene on behalf of a client; to urge an agency to change policies, practices, or regulations. In the field of mental health, the array of agencies that serve mentally ill persons have a broad perspective on the basic problem and thus have approaches and policies that differ and at times compete with one another. Some professionals contend that too much "advocacy" (e.g., providing transportation or brokering for a client to get into a job training program) can encourage dependency. Some argue that clients must be provided a wide latitude of choice and must be afforded an active role in their treatment arrangements. Client advocacy groups themselves often complain that they have not been consulted in the decisions that affect them and prefer not to be "advocated for" by what others see as benevolent persons. They prefer to advocate for themselves even though others define them as incompetent and thus unable to fight for their own cause.

All case management models contain elements of advocacy in their conceptualization (Weil and Karls, 1985). But can an agency, itself within the mental health system, successfully advocate for a client for improved or expanded services? With what authority can a mental health worker, even a professional, critique the system that funds the

jobs? The case management model is predicated on resource development and the combination of services to best suit a particular client's
needs. But how can a mental health worker in one agency insure that
needed housing from another agency will be available and accessible?
Frequently, external advocate agencies, using information from the
service providers, become the catalysts to bring about the needed
change. The use of law often is necessary to achieve social purposes
and redress current social program inadequacies.

OPERATIONAL ADVOCACY

Lourie (1975) suggests that the activities called advocacy must be
limited if they are to be realistic. He comments that while all expres-
sions of advocacy are important, their successes could well be futile
exercises without the fundamental rearrangements which are a prerequisite for successful change. He develops a concept called "operational advocacy," which he defines as the presence of a system or
systems of delivering human services focusing on ease of access at
local, neighborhood levels; that is, a more rational and accessible set
of human service systems. It seeks to find ways to integrate and
coordinate planning and services by interdisciplinary, intergroup,
inter-system communication. The purpose is to produce more effective approaches to implementation of the many objectives inherent in
human service. Operational advocacy "would require considerable
restructuring and coalescing of resources, forces and systems. It
would mean rearranging delivery systems so that the present
'farmer's market' set of services is converted to a 'supermarket'; a
rational flow of goods and services to the consumer rather than a set
of stalls from which he chooses at random" (Lourie:87).

For the seriously mentally ill, the "farmer's market" arrangement
of services is particularly ironic. While mental health professionals
often argue that these clients are unable to make treatment decisions
in their own best interest due to the unstable nature of their illness—
the same professionals are the ones most active in designing the
supermarket system of services that presumes an active consumer,
alert and able to secure the most appropriate services available. This
inconsistency is pervasive throughout the service delivery system for
the seriously mentally ill. On the one hand, mental health professionals (often in alliance with family members) frequently define
mentally ill persons as incompetent and in need of protection and yet
these very same professionals have encouraged the privatizing of the
mental health system dollar that has resulted in the proliferation of
individual practitioners vying for the most healthy clients, with no

single nucleus of responsibility or focus of coordination. Thus, even where such responsibility is legally determined, the translation is usually incomplete.

THE ROLE OF THE ADVOCACY ORGANIZATIONS

What is clearly needed is a truly ecumenical movement among mental health professionals, consumers, social service agencies, advocacy groups, family members, professional associations, and any other group with self-interest concerned with improving the service system for mentally disabled people. While clearly desirable, is it possible to find some common ground? Persons and groups with a variety of self-interests must collaborate with a unified conviction on policy and services and together advocate for agreed upon system changes. The following chapters will examine several constituent efforts on behalf of the mentally ill.

8

The Positions (and Needs) of Mental Health Advocates

Ever since the early 1970s, there has been a dramatic confrontation between the mental health system and the legal system in the United States. Active litigation has substantially changed the experience of mental illness for hundreds of thousands of people, including mentally ill persons, their families, mental health professionals, attorneys, and society as a whole. Some call this era the "patients' rights revolution," due to the dramatic changes that have taken place in less than two decades. The courts have played a significant role in these changes, and the extent of public debate between the legislative and judicial branches of government around the issues of mental illness are unparalleled in American history.

Several crucially important issues have been decided by the courts during this time. There were many rulings from the federal courts related to the right of a mentally disabled person to treatment (Wyatt v. Stickney); treatment in the least restrictive environments (Dixon v. Weinberger); protection from forced administration of intrusive procedures (Kaimowitz v. Michigan Department of Mental Health); and protection from involuntary commitment to a mental institution without due process (Lessard v. Schmidt). And while most mental health advocates and advocacy groups see these developments as progressive moves, the advocates themselves actually competed with one another in a "tangle of tensions between competing values, between various professions, and among the branches of government" (Wald and Friedman, 1978:138). The advocacy groups all feel that they are responsible and interested in improving the services and programs for the mentally disabled, yet their different approaches have led to conflict and confusion. The very definition of advocacy has different meaning among advocacy groups for mentally ill persons. Milner (1986) contends that virtually every group or organization involved in mental health policy has described its activities as being advocacy on behalf of mentally ill persons. He suggests that the term *advocacy*, though never clearly defined, has powerful symbolic content. He goes on to suggest that this symbolic quality limits mental health policy makers from seeing the obvious differences in other groups' perspectives and approaches. This limitation has profound implications for the formulation and implementation of mental health policy. The advocacy movement itself has created an imbalance in the field of mental health; its disagreements and tensions may be one cause for the slow progress made in this field. Compared to mentally ill persons, policies for the developmentally disabled have had much more public support. Efforts at deinstitutionalization were joined with policies that insured that community support programs would be implemented as the person left the hospital and began life in the community. Constitutionally protected rights were easily insured and money followed the patient into the community. The family members of the developmentally disabled person, in concert with professionals, attorneys, and politicians, forged an effective coalition to provide for these handicapped persons and insure their safety with public money.

ADVOCACY OF RIGHTS AND ADVOCACY OF NEEDS

Alan Stone (1979), president of the American Psychiatric Association, clearly states that the APA's notion of advocacy is to champion the *medical needs* of patients. He goes on to explain that the lawyers' notion is to champion the *legal rights* of clients. Psychiatrists want the client to have the best treatment setting, whereas attorneys argue for the least restrictive environment (a term that has become a euphemism for almost anything other than a state hospital). Stone states that there is a dichotomy between the psychiatrists' wish for careful treatment and planning for the continuity of care versus the attorneys' rush for immediate deinstitutionalization and maximizing a person's liberty. And he notes that while psychiatrists are concerned about access to treatment, attorneys are concerned about stigma and the right to refuse treatment. The poles are conceptualized as the *medical model* versus the *legal model*.

Building on the civil rights successes of the 1960s, in which political action on behalf of disenfranchised groups brought about legal and social change, "advocacy" for many other causes was attempted. Consumer advocates such as Ralph Nader's "Raiders" demonstrated that while a single consumer has little power to make demands or gain restitution from a big company, consumers as a power block can indeed force concessions. Civil rights advocates used the successful organizing techniques that won more equal rights for American blacks with other minority ethnic groups and others experiencing discrimination (e.g., women, homosexuals, the handicapped, Vietnam veterans). Welfare rights activists and advocates made deep inroads into the stifling bureaucracy of the public welfare system and by using the courts, class action suits, the media, and civil disobedience advanced the needs and interests of the poor.

Stone (1979:820) concludes that advocacy efforts such as those described above worked because each group's needs and interests could be readily defined; the interests could be formulated as some legal right and the "legal adversary had a powerful opponent, an adversary who had something to lose. Without an adversarial struggle, the judge has no real ability to find a resolution that is balanced." He then suggests that none of these elements have been present in the litigation in the field of mental health. He criticizes the legal advocates for mentally ill persons as not seriously considering the "needs" of mentally ill persons—rather, "they have treated *rights* as if they constituted the *needs* of mentally ill persons" [emphasis added].

The underlying tone of Dr. Stone's discussion is that most of the legal advocacy on behalf of mentally ill persons is actually an assault on the psychiatric profession and its ability to practice. Louis Kopolow (1979), the chief of patients' rights and advocacy programs for NIMH, saw the increase in the patients' rights movement as a genuine concern about the appropriateness and quality of health care. He also felt that psychiatrists were often unduly defensive and unwilling even to acknowledge the possibility of professional abuses. Kopolow argued that while psychiatrists have been the traditional advocates for their patients, a new, flexible, and less paternalistic attitude was advisable. The view remained, however, that there was very little conflict of interest between a patient and his or her psychiatrist. Nonetheless, while advocating for a higher degree of involvement from psychiatrists in their relationships with clients, the issues surrounding how to treat a patient were not considered to be a consumer matter.

Both Stone and Kopolow summarize their concerns by recommending that psychiatrists must handle the rights revolution by getting themselves lawyers and learning to work with them. Stone forcefully argued that for the American Psychiatric Association "the central task of working with lawyers is to create new laws that will reverse the trend of making rights into needs" (Stone, 1979:822). He notes that the courts are beginning to see the tragic implications of denying proper care to those suffering from a severe mental illness and in need of treatment. To emphasize the need for psychiatrists to practice their profession "unhindered by time-wasting legal procedures," must be a goal of the APA (Stone, 1979:822).

ADVOCACY FOR WHOM?

While there is tremendous concern about the legal versus the mental health professional's approach to advocacy, a major question remains. Who exactly are these groups representing? Patients' rights groups rarely are composed of mentally ill persons. Civil liberty groups fighting for alternatives to involuntary commitments rarely have lived in a state hospital. But in the mid-1970s, another stream of advocacy activities emerged. Ex-patients began to organize. This movement has been called the mental patients' liberation movement (Milner, 1986). The most politically radical of these groups (i.e., the Network Against Psychiatric Abuse, Mental Patients' Liberation Front, The Alliance for Liberation of Mental Patients) view psychiatry as the adversary and see psychiatrists as the oppressor. Using political strategies such as consciousness raising, organizing, and political action techniques, this movement has focused both on securing and protecting patients' rights as well as developing alternatives to mental hospitals (Chamberlin, 1977). Borrowing from some liberationist ideology (Friere, 1972), these early patient and ex-patient groups stressed the need for mutual support and shared experiences in order to increase their political awareness. Later groups modeled themselves on self-help models and rejected any involvement with professionals, whether psychiatrists or lawyers. The self-help organizations attempted to work at two levels at once. Groups such as GROW, The Emotionally Handicapped Anonymous, and Manic Depressives Anonymous, focused on finding ex-patients, forming groups led by nonprofessional facilitators to involve themselves in nurturing group experiences. A major goal of these efforts was to help ex-patients develop support systems in the community, strengthening their social skills, and helping them enter a network of other ex-patients that would provide support for them in the community. The earlier, more radical groups were suspicious of any professional advocates, no matter how well meaning and seemingly benevolent. Judi Chamberlin (1977), an early leader in the liberation movement, clearly warns patients and ex-patients about the role and influence that an "advocate" from the mental health system may play. She suggests that such people from the system can never be a legitimate advocate for patients' rights. She warns that it is impossible for a professional from inside the mental health system or hospital structure to correctly understand and legitimately express the grievances of mentally ill persons. By virtue of the fact that mental health professionals cannot see even the possibility of the inhumane aspects of their own treatment technologies, they must not speak on behalf of patients and ex-patients. The patients' rights organizations for the first time in history were speaking out in large numbers about the deplorable treatment they were receiving in American mental institutions and they were being met with a receptive response from the general public. However, mental health professionals as a group met the legislative and litigious activity with disappointment and resentment.

THE EMERGING CONSUMER DEMANDS IN MENTAL HEALTH SERVICES

Kopolow (1979) writes that the demands of the mental patients' movement go far beyond efforts to assure humane treatment in institutions. He suggests that their demands go to the core issues of involuntary commitment to hospitals and the legitimacy of forced treatment. And these issues clearly focus on the major differences between the medical model approach to mental health practice and the liberation approach. Patient activist groups disagree with two principal arguments usually used by mental health professionals in defense of civil commitment: dangerousness and incompetence.

Dangerousness

The use of dangerousness (to oneself or others) as a criterion for civil commitment of mentally ill persons is rejected by the patient activists groups for several reasons. First, they assert that there is no evidence that a mental health professional (or any other person) is able to predict the likelihood of future dangerous behavior. The American Psychiatric Association designed an index to test for violence proneness and reported that if this index were put into practice, it would identify eight times as many false positives as true positives (APA, 1974). The actual frequency of violence among mentally ill persons is very rare. And with no accurate baseline studies to compare violent acts among mentally ill persons with such acts among any other group of people, the use of these criteria as a basis for involuntary hospitalization is seen as suspect. Furthermore, patient groups contend that mental health professionals can all too easily bend the meaning of the word *dangerousness*, and the description of dangerous behavior can be easily distorted in order to fit the state criteria for commitment. Patient advocate groups frequently describe episodes in which a patient's resistance to the authority of the psychiatrist is used as evidence of dangerousness to his or her interests. Argumentativeness, a "counterculture" lifestyle, or unconventional dress or hair are often used as a support for the argument that a person is dangerous to himself and as a criterion for commitment. Patient groups see these terms as relative to prevailing community standards, too broad and vague to protect their right to remain free and too easily manipulated by family members, psychiatrists, and judges to be used as the grounds for civil commitment.

Family member groups such as the National Alliance for the Mentally Ill (NAMI) freely admit that since the involuntary statutes have become so difficult to use to commit a person in need of hospitalization, they will perjure themselves by stating that their family member has struck them or engaged in a violent act in order to provide the necessary "evidence" that a person is indeed dangerous and in need of hospitalization. The tragic irony of this situation is that family members, who could be extremely helpful in the care and support of a mentally ill person, now see the legal protections won by mentally ill persons as impediments to obtaining necessary treatment, so they are actively subverting them. This has implications for future family involvement in treatment protocols and the likelihood of successful independent living for the ill person in the community. Most of the seriously mentally ill still live with their families, yet providing false evidence against a person in need of treatment in order to commit them involuntarily to a state hospital obviously strains the future relationship, particularly when the patient gets stabilized and is better able to assess his or her situation. The collusion between psychiatrists and family members to "put a person away" still frightens many patients and ex-patients. Many understand the powerless position they are in and remember that the power imbalance was the original basis for the due process protections so recently litigated. More money is being spent on judicially coercing mentally ill persons into the existing, but often inappropriate programs that exist than in developing more appropriate, community-based alternatives that could better meet their needs. This has been noted frequently by the Mental Health Association in its critiques of the government's poor performance in this field.

Competent to Make Decisions

A second area of contention between the psychiatric orientation and patient liberation groups is the question of whether a mentally ill person is competent to make a treatment decision for him or herself. Here the issue is whether a person has the right to refuse treatment deemed necessary by a psychiatrist. The principle that medical treatment cannot be administered to an adult without voluntary, informed consent (except in a life-threatening emergency situation) has been established in common law in the United States. The one exception to that rule is the involuntarily committed psychiatric patient.

The purpose of committing a person to a psychiatric institution is for treatment. The underlying reason for this action is that a patient is unable to recognize his or her own best interests and therefore needs a psychiatrist to act on his or her behalf. Cooperating with a treatment regimen (such as electroconvulsive therapy and/or antipsychotic medication, with known debilitating side effects) is seen by psychiatrists as a sign of increasing health, insight, and capacity to function (Kopolow, 1979). If a person objects to the recommended treatment regimen and/or denies the mental illness, this is often viewed as evidence of the pathology itself and the person then is deemed to need more sustained treatment, often including longer-term incarceration.

THE RIGHT TO REFUSE PSYCHOTROPIC MEDICATION

Many psychiatrists have been involved in the debates supporting the legal regulation of treatments such as aversive conditioning, psychosurgery, and encouraging the requirement of informed consent for electroconvulsive therapy. But an area in which the psychiatric profession has bonded together tightly is the prescription and re-quired administration of psychotropic medication. The use of anti-psychotic medications has become the mainstay of modern psychiatric treatment, thus the patient's right to refuse such medica-tion is seen as an infringement on psychiatrists' right to practice their trade—an issue not up for debate. Mental health professionals who complain that patients are "dying with their rights on" due to unrealis-tically stringent laws on involuntary hospitalization are now com-plaining that patients are "rotting with their rights on," referring to the plight of patients who can now be hospitalized but not treated with the most effective treatment technologies available.

Legally, psychiatric patients, whether voluntary or involuntary, had generally been considered both by statute and by clinic practice to be "globally incompetent" (Miller, 1987) by virtue of their hospitaliza-tion. But an outcome of the patients' rights revolution made it clear that patients lost none of their individual rights (except their physical liberty) when hospitalized. Later, some states specifically added the patient's right to refuse psychiatric treatment and medication. This issue is still being litigated in various courts and thus specific court decisions are not yet controlling in the majority of states. In 1985, an American Bar Association survey reported that in forty-one states there was no explicit provision for a right to refuse treatment. Ten states had a statutory provision requiring consent before medicating in nonemergency situations.

The arguments on each side of the involuntary medication issue are aligned with the differences between mental health professionals and attorneys. Critics of involuntary procedures contend that there is no justification to force medication into unwilling patients. They argue that the medication is mostly used for control rather than for treatment and that there is little evidence that mentally ill persons are incapable of making informed treatment decisions. Furthermore, they note that psychotropic drugs are mind-altering and that the side effects are unpleasant and unhealthy. Others contend that the benefits of these medications have been exaggerated and that involuntarily forcing medications into a person decreases his or her autonomy (Parry, 1985), is demeaning, and damages the patient-psychiatrist relationship.

Most mental health professionals reject these arguments completely and suggest that the right to refuse treatment makes no sense if a psychiatric patient is to exercise his or her right to treatment. They counter that the right to refuse medication is based on legal misconceptions of the actions and benefits of medication. Miller (1987) comments that the issue has become much more important among the advocates than the patients themselves. Milner (1986:4) reports that when mental health advocates were asked how they determined the validity of the interests of the individual they were representing, many seemed genuinely puzzled by the question. Indeed, empirical studies document that the "right" to refuse treatment is exercised by very few patients. The feared epidemic of patient refusals to take medication has not materialized. Some authors even suggest that the right of refusal has had therapeutic advantages by allowing patients to discuss issues about their treatment and many have gained a better understanding about the treatment protocols. Psychiatrists have also seen the benefit of adopting a more flexible and cooperative attitude in dealing with patients. Kopolow (1979) recommends a new advocacy role for psychiatrists. The "true" advocate role for a psychiatrist, "in keeping with the best tradition of mental health services," is less paternalistic and includes "a willingness to hear a patient out with an open mind, no matter how mistaken we might initially feel he is" (Kopolow, 1979:269–270). He goes on to encourage psychiatrist/advocates not merely to fight against the newer and more restrictive civil commitment laws, but to work for the development and implementation of less restrictive facilities for patients who may not now meet the standards for involuntary hospitalization. Psychiatrist/activists must assume an active clinical and service advocacy role, "for to fail to do so leaves patients with no choice but dependence on the legal profession to arrange treatment priorities" (Kopolow, 1979:269).

OTHER DISPUTES: THE COURTS VERSUS THE OTHER BRANCHES OF GOVERNMENT AS AGENTS OF REFORM

Most Americans avoided and denied the stories of the psychiatrically disabled and their "snake pit" residences that occasionally crept out and into the press. Frederick Weisman's documentary film *Titticut Follies* boldly portrayed the psychological and physical abuse of the criminally insane incarcerated in a Massachusetts prison for the insane. The very fact that a filmmaker could so easily record the frequent abuses by guards and other prisoners alarmed the viewers, but did little to encourage action or change public policy. Geraldo Rivera, then a reporter for a local New York television station, took cameras into an institution for the mentally retarded called Willowbrook and this publicity, coupled with many suits brought by parents and public interest attorneys, did alert the public to the horrors of institutional abuse. A distinction developed, however, between the tragic life circumstances of developmentally disabled "children" (even though many of the Willowbrook residents were not children) and mentally ill persons. Downs syndrome, which strikes families from all socioeconomic classes, is known to be a chromosomal disorder. These facts have reduced the stigma associated with mental retardation and has assisted the organization of parent/advocacy groups who now have become a politically powerful force capable of bringing about significant changes in public policy and protections to benefit the mentally retarded. Mentally ill persons, however, still lurk under the suspicion that they are in some way responsible for their plight and that their parents or family "caused" their illnesses. These beliefs have hampered the advocacy efforts on their behalf, and the reforms achieved to benefit them lag behind the mentally retarded. Before the 1970s, courts and attorneys rarely ventured into the civil mental health system. The first major case dealing with a patient's right was *Rouse v. Cameron*, in the District of Columbia in 1967. Mr. Rouse sued St. Elizabeth's Hospital because he was receiving no treatment but had been found "not guilty by reason of insanity" and was being held indefinitely since he was incompetent to stand trial. The American Psychiatric Association issued a position statement following the Rouse decree maintaining that the appraisal of adequate treatment was a matter of medical determination. This started a dispute between the psychiatric establishment's avowed authority to practice its trade unfettered by "outside community agencies" and the court's attempts to protect the rights of committed psychiatric patients under the U. S. Constitution. Little actual improvement in treatment and facilities took place, but a new era of "judicial activism" began.

Judicial Activism for the Psychiatric Patient

Starting in the early 1970s, a spate of cases on behalf of the mentally ill were being taken to court. The development of a mental health bar, initially within various branches of the American Civil Liberties Union, culminated in the establishment of the Mental Health Law Project. This national organization, based in Washington, D. C., provides advocacy and consultation to attorneys. A group of well-trained, active attorneys began taking, appealing, and winning constitutional challenges to the existing procedural protections. The legal philosophy of the Warren Court and its influence on the other federal courts led to an activism not seen before.

The term *judicial activism* became a household word during the Senate confirmation hearings of President Reagan's nominee, Robert Bork, to fill a vacancy on the Supreme Court. Much of the public debate, which was televised and viewed by millions, centered on whether justices of the Supreme Court should limit their activities to classical interpretations of the Constitution and avoid attempts to modernize its original intent. Judge Bork, a widely acclaimed constitutional scholar, was not confirmed by the Senate primarily due to his conservative stance and seemingly unsympathetic point of view on civil rights.

However, for almost twenty years, judges in lower federal courts had been actively altering the rights of mentally ill persons by requiring states to provide them with better treatment and to insure that the state institutions that housed them were humane.

In 1971, Judge Frank Johnson, after personally visiting a state institution for mentally ill persons in Alabama, found that the hospital setting itself was so deplorable that it was an unconstitutional deprivation of the rights of patients to be "treated" there (Wyatt v. Stickney, 1971). He contended that any person involuntarily committed to a state institution must receive adequate and effective treatment as the basic minimum to justify a person's commitment. Other court rulings began detailing specific requirements, such as staff ratios, food and space allotments, etc., as the minimum requirements to insure a patient's right to treatment. These rulings all followed the philosophy that if the state deprived a person of the liberty for the sake of treatment, there must be evidence of treatment being carried out. It was later specified in a D. C. court, that this treatment must take place in the least restrictive environment possible (see Lake v. Cameron). Some courts began requiring states to provide alternatives to hospitalizations even when none were presently available. A California Supreme Court in 1985 concluded that there is no constitutional right to community mental health treatment in the least restrictive environment. Yet a Denver Probate Court ruled that while chronically mentally ill persons have a right under Colorado statutes to care and treatment in the community in the least restrictive environment, there are no such rights under the Federal Community Mental Health Centers Act, the Rehabilitation Act, or under common law. The Supreme Court is now giving signs that it no longer desires judicial intervention in the professional decisions being made at the state level (Miller, 1987).

Wald and Friedman (1978) note that the Wyatt case provided an excellent illustration of the tensions between judicial and legislative (or executive) reform. The State of Alabama on its appeal of the Wyatt case argued that the court decree constituted an illegal infringement upon the functions of the state legislature. Lawyers defending the state contended that the governor and the legislature, justly alarmed by the high costs of implementing the newly mandated minimum standards with limited state resources, are the ones responsible for balancing the needs of mentally ill persons against the needs of other equally worthy citizens. They argued that the court should not interfere with that process. But the circuit court held that many constitutionally based decisions require an expenditure of funds and that lack of adequate financial resources was not acceptable as a justification for the denial of a constitutional right. Thus, the debate goes on.

Mental Health Advocacy and the Political Process

Patient advocate groups traditionally go to their state legislatures first to request more money for their causes. They bring documented evidence and argue for the need to change policies, fund new initiatives, and shift legislative priorities. When this doesn't work satisfactorily, patient advocate groups turn to the court for help. Public interest attorneys, taking class action suits on behalf of an aggrieved person, attempt to win cases or get settlement decrees from the various states that mandate changes and require that more money be put into state institutions for improved services and programs for mentally ill persons. What has not yet been clarified, however, is this: What if the states refuse to comply with a court-ordered decree? How much power does a federal court have over the priority setting of a state legislature? How can the courts monitor the states, and is it their role to do so? How will a court get accurate information that a mandated decree is indeed being implemented?

THE PROTECTION AND ADVOCACY LAW FOR
MENTALLY ILL PEOPLE

While court rulings in recent years have begun to reverse the trend to protect individual rights against state's rights in the mental health field, Congress, in 1986, enacted Public Law 99–319, The Protection and Advocacy for Mentally Ill Individuals Act. This legislation stemmed from an investigation of conditions in state mental hospitals conducted in 1984 by the Senate Subcommittee on the Handicapped. The study documented numerous instances of abuse and neglect of patients in institutions. This legislation funds advocacy services for mentally ill people in each state. With the passage of this law, the federal government expanded its role in funding advocacy for disadvantaged people. Protection and advocacy programs were already established for persons with developmental disabilities, severely handicapped people receiving rehabilitation services, and the elderly.

Public Law 99–319 provides funds to the states for advocacy agencies with the authority to investigate incidents of abuse and neglect of mentally ill persons and to pursue administrative, legal, and other appropriate remedies to protect mentally ill people. No new rights are established under the law, but it provides funds for advocacy services to protect existing state, federal, and constitutional rights. Funds appropriated under this act were distributed to every state. Each state received a minimum of $125,000, with more determined by a formula based on population and per capita income. Neglect of a person with a significant mental illness or emotional impairment is defined as "a negligent act or omission by any individual responsible for providing services in a facility rendering care or treatment which causes or may have caused injury to a mentally ill individual or places a mentally ill individual at risk or injury, and includes . . . the failure to establish or carry out an appropriate individual program plan or treatment plan for a mentally ill individual, the failure to provide adequate nutrition, clothing, or health care to a mentally ill individual or the failure to provide a safe environment for a mentally ill individual." Neglect also includes discharge without appropriate treatment plans and services, and the failure to inform mentally ill persons of available community services.

TENSIONS AMONG THE MENTAL HEALTH ADVOCATES

Psychiatrists trained before the 1960s presumed that their work with mentally ill persons would focus on clinical diagnoses and treatment interventions. Few anticipated the dramatic changes in the practice of psychiatry brought about by changes in the laws and court decisions. Challenges emerged to such basic questions as who is mentally ill, who is in need of treatment, when is a person likely to become dangerous, who should take antipsychotic medications, and when should persons be treated against their will. These challenges were coming from patients, advocates, family members, and other aligned mental health professionals. Many psychiatrists and other mental health professionals see "active adversarial attorneys and militant former patients . . . [as attacking] both the existence of mental illness and the ability of psychiatrists to diagnose and treat it" (Miller, 1987:xv). Clinicians, attorneys, and civil rights activists see the basic issues surrounding the definitions and treatment arrangements for mentally ill persons differently. Clinicians frequently see attorneys as primarily concerned with the procedures, methods, and legal principles of a case, rather than with the actual outcomes for an individual client. Attorneys see clinicians as overly confident about the impact of their treatment modalities and insufficiently concerned about the rights and choices of their patients. Civil rights activists are most concerned about the potential loss of a patient's liberties ensuing from the psychiatric treatment itself as well as the consequences and focus on protections for mentally ill persons. Each perspective views the other with alarm and at times these points of view come into severe conflict. These differences are clearly seen in the public debates over changing laws and administrative procedures, as well as what is considered the public mandate to care for mentally ill persons.

Over the last two decades, clinicians themselves have begun to examine their assumptions about what behavior sufficiently justifies depriving someone of liberty in the name of treatment. The category of mental disorders for which involuntary treatment is justified has been narrowed and has become more clearly defined through behavioral attributes. Now, the model commitment statute proposed by the American Psychiatric Association defines a severe mental disorder as "an illness, disease, organic brain disorder, or other condition that (1) substantially impairs the person's thought, perception of reality, emotional distress, or judgment or (2) substantially impairs behavior as manifested by recent disturbed behavior." However, most courts continue to be primarily concerned with the issue of "dangerousness" and in practice are less concerned with the evidence for mental illness, regardless of how it is defined (Hiday, 1977). Another interesting trend is that while civil rights activists criticize psychiatrists for their broad latitude in defining mental illness, for fear that persons not mentally ill will be involuntarily committed, many clinicians themselves are concerned that the courts are committing people who meet the dangerousness criteria, but are "nontreatable" persons in terms of currently available psychiatric treatment modalities. Thus they complain that the courts are filling the hospitals with persons who interfere with the effective treatment of other truly mentally ill persons who could benefit from known psychiatric interventions.

By 1970, every state had revised its statutes to include either "dangerous to oneself or dangerous to others" as one necessary criterion for a civil commitment. By 1983, twelve states required evidence of clear physical danger or an identifiable act to meet the dangerousness standard. Almost every other had included it as one of the criteria in its commitment statutes. However, the ability of a psychiatrist to predict a person's likelihood of becoming dangerous has been severely challenged by recent studies. So has the notion that a mentally ill person is more likely than anyone else to commit an act of violence. A study conducted by the American Civil Liberties Union concluded that "it now seems beyond dispute that mental health professionals have *no* special expertise in predicting dangerous behavior either to oneself or to others. In fact, predictions of dangerousness are wrong about 95 percent of the time" (Ennis, 1978). Yet many courts, regardless of statutory changes requiring the dangerousness criteria, continue to assume that mentally ill persons are dangerous to themselves solely by virtue of their disorders. And many judges continue to believe that clinicians are the most appropriate persons to make recommendations to the court concerning commitments of mentally ill persons even though their ability to predict dangerousness is poor (Hiday, 1971).

Again, different groups of professionals have reacted with different positions to the requirement that dangerousness be predictable before commitment may be ordered. Most mental health professionals have rejected dangerousness as a necessary element for commitment for a variety of reasons. Many mental health professionals believe that dangerousness, as such, is not a clinical construct and that the purpose of involuntary hospitalization (or any treatment modality) is to provide effective treatment to mentally ill persons. Some psychiatrists openly suggest that dangerous patients may not be treatable and are merely using up scarce time and resources that would be better spent with other types of clients who are amenable to treatment. Still others assert that there are many seriously mentally ill persons who are *treatable* and who would not meet the dangerousness criteria, but who reject voluntary treatment and thus go without treatment, though they would have benefited from such interventions.

Attorneys and civil rights advocates contend that the inclusion of the dangerousness criteria for civil commitment is necessary as a protection against "indiscriminant commitment based on legally, unreviewable clinical judgments" (Mulvey and Lidz, 1985). If a person's behavior is not showing a significant risk to that person or to any other person, the state should not be permitted to exercise its considerable powers against that person by requiring incarceration for treatment. The federal court in Hawaii, in *Susuki v. Quisenberry* (1976), clearly rejected the clinical authority as the sole basis for commitment. It held that the diagnosis and treatment of mental illness leaves too much to subjective choices by less than neutral individuals to be acceptable in proceedings in which a person may lose his or her liberty. Later, the Hawaii legislature revised its commitment laws to require that if the courts find "beyond a reasonable doubt" that a individual is "likely" to do substantial injury to another, he or she may be civilly committed.

THE POLAR POSITIONS

The service advocates and the civil rights advocates perhaps differ most strongly around the issue of civil commitment. The very reason for its existence is debated between these two groups. The "police power" used to protect society from the acts of dangerous persons is contrasted with the "parental power" which focuses on the need to treat and help persons in need. These two justifications for civil commitment in most states form the framework of the argument between these groups.

The Civil Libertarian Perspective

The civil libertarians believe that whatever presumed benefits of mental health treatment a person may obtain, there is also potential for major harm due to the loss of liberty when one is hospitalized involuntarily. They compare the commitment of a mentally ill person to the incarceration of a convicted criminal and see little actual difference, since they both lose their physical freedom, may be living in wards with no privacy, may be forced to take medication, and are subject to other potentially hazardous and intrusive procedures. Total institutions are frequently brutalizing, disruptive to a person's ability to maintain contact with his or her family and friends, and potentially disruptive to a person's employment; after even a short period of institutionalization, it is often difficult to socially reintegrate the person successfully back into the community (Segal and Aviram, 1978). The position that civil commitment is "for a patient's own good" is a suspect premise among civil libertarians. The right to be deviant must be protected or else there is a danger that any unusual lifestyle or ideology may be used to enforce the values of the majority. The question becomes: Does the state have the power to put away harmless mentally ill people solely because the public is uncomfortable when exposed to them? These advocates contend that unless a person is clearly physically dangerous, the state has no legitimate purpose in confining him or her and imposing treatment against his or her will. Some critics of this approach note that while arguing for a strict criterion of dangerousness to be put into state laws, these groups also argue that there is no way to predict future dangerous behavior, so their true motive is to halt all involuntary commitments.

The Service-Oriented Perspective

Many mental health professionals and service-oriented advocates answer that most people treated with brief hospitalizations are indeed significantly improved when released and should not be denied these treatment technologies when they are too sick to know they need them. They want to see the grounds for involuntary treatment to be the probability of help, not danger to society. In fact, most mental health experts testify that their skills are most effective with treatable, mentally ill persons, not a dangerous person being committed against his or her will. But while acknowledging that many seriously mentally ill persons can successfully be treated in community-based programs, there are not enough of them in most states. Thus, it is not appropriate to dump people from the hospitals to the streets with no supports and every likelihood of becoming unable to cope with the indignities of urban street life. They complain that since there is no constitutional right to adequate and effective mental health treatment in the community on a voluntary basis, the only way to get people the "right" to be treated with known, effective services is to commit them to a psychiatric facility involuntarily. Some see this as a tragic irony. Others, however, see the parallel with certain medical procedures that are covered by Medicare or Medicaid insurances when conducted in a hospital, but not when done in an outpatient facility (regardless of the fact that the outpatient procedure is usually far less costly). Service-oriented advocates contend that if the commitment criteria are restricted to cases involving imminent danger of serious bodily harm to oneself or others, based on a recent overt act, society would have no authority to intervene in the lives of most of the persons with serious mental illnesses today.

INTRACTABLE POSITIONS?

While the two groups seem to be at opposite sides of the mental health spectrum, at times there is common ground, or at least they can find overlapping zones of agreement around which to find compromise.

Wald and Friedman (1978) use the Bryce Hospital case in Alabama as an example of an interesting compromise among the competing interest advocates. Mental health professionals and attorneys held several strategy sessions preceding the *Wyatt v. Stickney* right-to-treatment litigation. There was no dispute that the staff of three part-time psychiatrists, two social workers, and one psychologist for the 5,000 patients who resided in Bryce Hospital was inadequate. No one disagreed that the physical plant was deplorable and many considered it to be dangerous. At this point, however, positions diverged.

Those coming from the mental health perspective felt these conditions required immediate action and that the court must find a constitutional right to treatment with mandatory minimum standards to prevent physical harm and to insure adequate therapy and rehabilitation. The civil rights perspective, while aware of the plight of the patients living at Bryce Hospital, felt that right-to-treatment litigation would legitimate state hospitals generally and thus serve indirectly to increase the use of involuntary hospitalization. The polar positions seemed intractable.

But by looking at the *needs* of each group, rather than the stated *positions*, a compromise could be forged and both groups were satisfied. The needs of the service-oriented perspective focused on better conditions within Bryce Hospital. To them there could be no compromise that would delay further this deplorable situation. On the one side, there was the fear that improving the facility and staff ratio of the hospital would result in a vast increase in the use of civil commitment, further depriving seriously mentally ill people their liberty. A compromise was possible. It was pointed out that substantially increasing the costs of hospitalization by improving its physical plant, staffing patterns, and programs, would both benefit the residents inside and probably serve as a *disincentive* to the state to pay for unnecessary commitments (in favor, one hopes, of less costly community-based services as an alternative).

Another example of finding zones of agreements between the advocate adversaries is around the issue of providing mental health treatments in the least restrictive environment. This debate has centered on many courts' rulings that there is a constitutional basis for requiring commitment to take place in the least restrictive environment possible. While the benefits of this seem obvious, civil libertarians fear that such activities as daily visits by mental health professionals into the homes of ex-patients or the establishment of guardians for mentally ill persons unwilling to be involved in some type of program could easily result in an overextension of the state into the lives of mentally ill persons. The service-oriented advocates see these suits as necessary for them to obtain leverage in securing the much needed range of community-based services as alternatives to institutionalization.

9

Finding the Zones of Agreement

NEGOTIATING THE NEEDS OF MENTALLY ILL PEOPLE

In an elegantly simple but profound book called *Getting to Yes* (1983), Roger Fisher and William Ury describe a process of negotiation in which parties in a dispute can both win without feeling that they have given in. While perhaps not conceptualized this way before, mental health professionals, family members of mentally ill people, civil rights attorneys, hospital personnel, state and government workers, politicians, and mentally ill people themselves are all engaging frequently in negotiating the realities of mental health, mental illness, and the organizational and professional systems designed to meet the ongoing service delivery challenge. These negotiations include not only the arguments and debates about what mental illness is and what causes it (as described in Chapter 7), but finding the appropriate intervention strategies, defining who is responsible for taking the problem at the crisis stage or the long-term care stage, who pays, who has the ultimate authority for bringing about beneficial changes, and who is responsible when the changes do not occur or negative results occur.

Issues are being negotiated daily throughout the fifty states. Where does one's personal responsibility end and the state or local government's begin? Is mental illness an individual's problem or perhaps the family's—or is it a collective responsibility, with federal, state, and local parameters? What level of government should assume the responsibility for seriously mentally ill people? Should states be allowed to determine the funding levels and programmatic support for the mentally ill within their own priorities, or should a national program (or national minimums) exist? Should entitlement programs and insurance such as Medicaid, SSDI, and SSI provide medical care and income to these disabled persons? Should the insurance beneficiary be free (or required) to locate his or her own services wherever they exist in the community (from either private or public vendors), or should public programs be specifically designed for these people? Seriously and persistently mentally ill people today often have to negotiate their own living arrangements as they are being moved out of the state hospitals that had long been their homes and reintegrated into a community. Frequently they are negotiating with their SSI dollars to pay for boarding and care home rents, or more typically for the nursing home in which they now live. Family members of adult children diagnosed as schizophrenics need to negotiate long-term services with careful financial protections built in so that as they age, their adult but ill children will be assured continuing care and services. Mental health professionals and private service providers negotiate usually lucrative purchase-of-service contracts with the state mental health departments to provide, in the private sector, the services mandated by the state legislatures. And state mental health workers negotiate with their departments (and sometimes unions) for adequate pay, safe working conditions, and reasonable case loads; and they request reasonable laws, policies, and treatment technologies so they can provide adequate services to their clients.

In order to find "zones of agreement" around which these different actors to the negotiation process can build consensus, it is important to "hear" the positions, interests, and needs of each. Fisher and Ury (1983) make an important distinction between *positions* and *interests*. *Interests* involve needs, desires, concerns, and fears. *Positions* are the things you have decided upon, based on your interests. However, by looking past the positions and into the interests (both one's own and others'), solutions to problems may be found. Frequently, behind opposing positions lie shared and compatible interests (as well the more easily identified and articulated conflicting ones).

While advocates for the mentally ill are not new (see Chapter 7 for discussion), two new groups have become prominent recently—the National Alliance for the Mentally Ill and the psychiatrically disabled consumers themselves. These groups, along with the Mental Health Association, the Offices of Protection and Advocacy, and the American Civil Liberties Union, all have become active advocates for the needs of the seriously mentally ill. But the voices from these groups are far from harmonious. In fact, they often loudly criticize one another and have diametrically opposed each others' policy proposals, legislative actions, and even philosophy.

The National Alliance for the Mentally Ill (NAMI)

NAMI is a national group of over 500,000 members made up primarily of families with mentally ill relatives. Since its inception in 1979, its goals have been fairly consistent.

Self-help: Support and Education for Families   Most of the people active in the NAMI groups say that it is their need for support and information that first brought them together (Hatfield, 1987:200–203). Most NAMI meetings across the country begin with time set aside for "sharing and caring." In a spirit of togetherness, NAMI members share their experiences of family life with their psychiatrically disabled family member and hear similar reports from others in a sympathetic atmosphere. Most members say that these discussions help them feel less alone and more hopeful and that they learn new ideas for managing their problems from the others. The self-help function is a primary one for NAMI. Its phenomenal growth over the last decade clearly demonstrates that a vein of need is being tapped for these families, where previously no one had been helping them in this way.

In her research of family members of seriously mentally ill adults in Hawaii, Barbara Digman (1987) found that learning about mental illness was a primary concern. Traditionally, mental health professionals have left the families with adult children who are mentally ill out of the information "loop." This has been a particularly severe problem for families with children who have been diagnosed as schizophrenic. The onset of the illness many not fully manifest itself until the late teen years, just as the child is expected to become independent from the family. And although problems may have been identified earlier, rarely is a family prepared for the devastating reality of schizophrenia. The lack of precise information given to most family members, even though they are often the primary caregivers for the ill person, is particularly frustrating, irritating, and demoralizing (Digman, 1987).

Reeducation of Mental Health Professionals   An important goal of NAMI is to change the attitudes and knowledge base of currently practicing mental health professionals through reeducation and influence on the training and education of the new entrants into the profession. NAMI documents the evidence that many mental health professionals feel uncomfortable with seriously mentally ill patients and many do not feel positive about their family members. Early psychoanalytic and psychodynamic theories focused heavily on the role of the family members in the onset of schizophrenia. Many family members feel that they are being blamed for their child's illness and that their strengths are being ignored. NAMI has collected and is developing the most recent research available on the biochemical aspects of schizophrenia and wants to inform the professionals what it is *really* like to have a loved one become mentally ill and all the stresses that event brings to the family.

Advocacy   NAMI has become a loud voice alerting the public to the catastrophic proportions that a diagnosis of mental illness brings to the family. Few families have the resources necessary to provide even a minimal level of care and support that the ill person needs. And society rarely has the appropriate facilities and programs even if one had the money to buy them. Poor housing, poor hospital care, and poorly organized treatment systems are what most family members face as they search daily for help with their disabled family member. NAMI provides families with a powerful vehicle for advocating for changes in the mental health system.

Family Advocacy   The policy of deinstitutionalization substantially reduced the numbers of seriously mentally ill people residing for long periods of time (often a lifetime) in state psychiatric hospitals. It was premised on the idea that these people would be returned to their communities. But study after study consistently reveals that the single most critical factor which prevents effective service coordination and implementation of rational discharge planning is the lack of provision for adequate specialized housing for the chronically disabled (Baxter and Hooper, 1984). Thus, most of the seriously mentally ill people in the United States live with their families and the costs to these families are immense. Stigma has prevented these family members from "complaining" or speaking out on the psychological stress and economic strain that a seriously ill person becomes on the family. However, recently there has been a dramatic change in the willingness of family members to assert themselves into the public arena and tell their stories to mental health professionals, legislators, mental health policy makers, and the public. At its 1982 annual convention, the National Alliance for the Mentally Ill chose the theme "Empowering Consumers of Mental Health Services." Its emphasis was on consumer education. This approach, modeled on the civil rights movement and the women's movement, intended to "arm individuals with the knowledge and self-confidence needed to make choices which can increase individual satisfaction, marketplace efficiency, and the public good" (Hatfield, 1984:320).

Why Family Advocacy Now?   An intriguing part of this new advocacy movement is that it is based on the rights of family members, *not* the primary consumer. There are several reasons why this movement developed. Due to the decreasing population in the state hospitals, the responsibility for the care and shelter for most of the seriously and persistently mentally ill has returned to the families. The lives of family members have changed irrevocably as they have taken on the burdens of caregiving. And since many of these families are caring for adults (either children, siblings, or spouses)—who may be quite disturbed, disruptive, and disturbing—they have little leverage with which to require treatment, obtain service, or achieve improved behavior. Second, with the growth of the patients' rights movement, most families feel extremely frustrated at their inability to obtain treatment for their family member until he or she has become so sick and disabled that the mental health system will seek involuntary hospitalization based on the person's dangerous behavior. Many families decry a system that buffets them between state deinstitutionalization policies to keep the hospital bed census down, civil rights legislation that makes involuntary institutionalization difficult to accomplish, insufficient housing options in the community, and few community-based treatment/residential alternatives. An emerging gap between the families and the mental health providers developed. The families have clearly articulated their dissatisfaction with the professionals' theories that blame the families for the causes of the manifestations of schizophrenia. They also complain about the professionals' insensitivity to the burdens of life with a seriously and persistently psychiatrically disabled person. Family members who meet in self-help groups are gaining courage to resist family therapy models that tend to focus responsibility for the family's dysfunctions, inadequacies, and peculiarities on the parents. Now family members are telling mental health professionals to focus on their strengths, help them to cope, teach them useful behavioral management techniques, and stop blaming them for the illness of the family member. Family members have begun demanding accurate, current, and empirically valid information about schizophrenia from mental health professionals and are quite critical of those unable or unwilling to provide it to them. Families are now demanding concrete skill-management techniques rather than psychodynamic theories (most of which had never been demonstrated to be effective with seriously mentally ill people). Family members are now demanding respite from society and financial relief from the constant caregiving they are providing. Whereas the state hospitals previously provided the total care for society's seriously mentally ill, now the burden has returned to the families, with the dollars for treatment rarely following the patient into the family's budget. With this new burden has come a new form of advocacy and it is anticipated that they will become a potent voice with significant leverage on the policy development of mental health issues over the next few years.

Consumer Orientations: The Families' Needs

Agnes Hatfield has become a champion of those who are caring for a relative who is seriously mentally ill. Her writings and personal experiences as well as her active participation in the development of the National Alliance for the Mentally Ill has made her a publicly acclaimed spokesperson for the newly emerging family advocacy movement. She has recently turned her attention to the development of training materials for mental health professions and is presently staff coordinator for NAMI's curriculum and training projects. Her considerable knowledge, experience and influence is reflected in the following section.

THE NEED FOR RESPITE

Family members who have organized themselves into self-help groups clearly articulate a common concern—they need respite from the exhausting, burdensome task of caregiving. The devastation that family members experience when confronting a diagnosis of schizophrenia (or other serious psychosis) has profound implications psychologically, financially, and socially. An often heard problem is the lack of respite from the daily burdens involved in the care of a seriously ill person. And while relatives of ill children with cystic fibrosis, cancer, or even mental retardation experience deep pain and suffering, the families of the mentally ill, primarily due to the unknowns about the etiology and course of the disease, face uncertainty with a unknown future. Relatives can rarely plan for future events, because they can not predict the condition of their ill family member. Relatives frequently choose not to leave home for vacations or holidays, because they do not know if their ill family member may need them or if they can safely leave them in the community. Family members rarely entertain in their home, because they fear that the behavior of their ill relative may be disruptive. Thus, the pattern for family members becomes one of little or no respite, little or no leisure activities with the healthy family members, and the numbing realization that no alternative is in sight. Many NAMI chapters are now focusing on the problem of the aging family member (usually a parent) who can not and will not be able to look toward their "golden" years of retirement as a time to reap the rewards of earlier accomplishments. Rather, for these families, the future is a frightening scenario of what will happen to their ill child as the parents age and become less able to provide the caregiving? This fear pervades the self-help movement.

The Need for Financial Relief

The thought that plagues many relatives of seriously mentally ill is the constant financial expenses incurred due to the illness. The constant expenses of the current medical and psychiatric costs of the illness and the fear that there will be no end in sight is a huge problem for the relatives. Whereas most family members look to the day when their children grow up and become independent, family members of chronically mentally ill people quickly give up on that expectation; it is replaced with the reality that the financial drain of treating and housing an ill person will be a lifetime burden.

Financing care for the seriously mentally ill is particularly problematic for relatives attempting to assist with the bills since deinstitutionalization. The current financing picture shows a vast array of funding sources—private, state, and federal—but coverage is spotty, fragmented, and with a focus on inpatient care and acute episodes of illness. This is not the common situation of the chronically psychiatrically disabled.

The Drain of the State Hospitals   The direct state allocations to build, maintain, and operate hospitals for the mentally ill, although declining in importance, still represent a visible and costly form of care that absorbs a high percentage of states' funds. While the number of state hospitals, the number of people living in them, and the number of days spent per patient are all declining, the cost of maintaining this form of care has increased almost three-and-a-half times during the last fifteen years, draining money away from the needed community-based services (Rubin, 1987). Some suggest that the mandated improvement of care has increased the cost per patient of inpatient care even though the numbers served decreased. Others suggest that political constraints such as union contracts, governmental construction, and state operational arrangements have resulted in the justification for keeping state hospitals open. It is true, however, that after deinstitutionalization, the residents left in the hospitals were the most severely ill, often with both medical and psychiatric disabilities, thus keeping the costs of care for this small segment of the population high. State support to the community-based mental health system is usually given directly to the provider of the service and is severely underfunded, and the wide array of private services is often difficult for the severely disabled to successfully negotiate. Many charge that the "worried well" or the "unhappy healthy" draw both the attention and funds from the state away from the most seriously mentally ill, leaving them few treatment choices and still fewer residential alternatives which they can afford.

Federal Insurance and Public Assistance   The federal government provides insurance and assistance in several ways: Social Security Disability Insurance (SSDI), Supplemental Security Income (SSI), Medicaid, Medicare, and through the Veterans Administration (VA). Most are not well suited to meeting the needs of the seriously mentally ill. For example, many mentally ill individuals may work for periods of time between episodes of illnesses. This intermittent work record, however, often disqualifies a SSDI or SSI recipient and at times even from Medicaid and Medicare. Inpatient care, reimbursed by Medicaid and Medicare programs, may be inappropriate, whereas social rehabilitation and case management services are not easily reimbursed by the federal programs. The financial incentives often push people into inappropriate alternatives. For example, Medicaid will pay for lengthy stays in nursing homes, but the focus is on medical conditions, and services can not include specialized services like psychiatric interventions. Thus this transinstitutionalization from psychiatric hospital to nursing home occurs only because the care is reimbursable and there is a lack of community services and housing. Medicaid reimbursements for nursing care make this type of care a necessary choice (although an expensive and often inappropriate one, if other alternatives were available and reimbursable).

Private Insurance and the Families' Costs   Talbott and Sharfstein (1986) suggest that between 49 and 65 percent of the 1.7–2.4 million chronically mentally ill people live with their families. Dependents of employed workers may be covered for certain mental health services through their employer's health insurance plan. Usually the benefits are quite restrictive and limited. Most commonly, there is a limit on the total lifetime costs that an insurer will pay for mental health treatment or a total lifetime number of days in treatment. The deductibles and coinsurance for mental health services are usually substantially higher than those for other health care costs. Frequently there are restrictions on the type of provider the insurer will reimburse. Even the most carefully insured family often is faced with the unhappy choices of having to spend large sums of money to finance the care needed, attempt to have their relative institutionalized, or find a way to have the relative qualify for welfare assistance. Even when insurance coverage is available, the fiscal incentives are such that there are clear biases towards institutional care in medically oriented settings even though other types of care are more appropriate and less expensive. This problem stems from the fact that most insurance arrangements are adaptations of the basic health insurance model based on physical illnesses. The issues and needs surrounding mental illnesses are quite different and need different types of care and services and thus different types of insurance protection. These are rarely found and the financial burden remains primarily with the relatives of the disabled person.

Psychological Relief

Another common theme heard from the family advocates is that mental health professionals are insensitive to family members' needs, are not helpful, and withhold from them crucial information about their relative. (They also note that most professionals rarely request information from them about their ill relative or even listen to their concerns, which most family members believe would be helpful data for the professional to use in his or her assessment.)

Of particular concern is the fact that family members frequently come into contact with mental health professionals who have been trained with a family therapy perspective that sees the family and its dynamics and organizational structure as a causal agent in the development of schizophrenia. Until very recently, the attitudes of many mental health professionals toward families of the chronically mentally ill have been on the whole negative and uncooperative (Potasznik and Nelson, 1984). Professionals have held certain biases about mental illness that have precluded objective analysis and appropriate treatment. For example, many therapists want to examine the organizational structure of the family in order to understand the role the mentally ill person plays in the family (see Haley, 1980; Madanes, 1981). Others believe that family relationships are detrimental to the person with schizophrenia—specifically the interactions patterns and the mother-child relationship (Falloon, Boyd and McGill, 1984). Many mental health practitioners patently see the role of the therapist as the expert and knowledge holder and are unwilling to share information, insights, or "family secrets" with relatives. The world view of these therapists is one of family disorganization and disordered communication (Wynne et al., 1978); some studies have suggested that all schizophrenics come from emotionally disturbed families (Lidz, 1973). Clearly this perspective, which comes close to blaming the families for the suffering of their relative, is a difficult perspective for families to accept. These negative attitudes reinforce the existing states of anxiety, stress, and guilt already in these families. Furthermore, it is unlikely that these family members will seek help from such therapists, nor see them as helpful allies. Ironically, recent research has begun to demonstrate that families that do not have good information about the symptoms and realistic expectations about their relative's disorder are more critical and upset when symptoms are displayed, which in turn results in a poorer prognosis for the disabled person living in such families.

Expressed Emotion   The most recent and influential theory gaining popularity among mental health practitioners is the theory of expressed emotion (EE). This area of research has focused on exploring relationships between family members' attitudes and the progress of their relative's rehabilitation. Leff's (1986) findings indicate that persons with schizophrenia are extremely sensitive to their social environments and particularly aware and alert to the behaviors and attitudes of their family members. These investigations have found that relapses of schizophrenia, specifically recurrence or exacerbation of symptoms, occur at a greater rate among patients whose family members exhibit hostility or criticism toward the ill relative. Emotional warmth, however, has been associated with improvement in the ill person's condition after hospital discharge (Leff, 1986). Investigators have concluded that expressed emotion, as measured by an index comprising factors assessing the number of critical comments, hostile or negative remarks, emotional overinvolvement, warmth, praise, and approval, is the strongest predictor of symptomatic relapse during the first nine months after hospital discharge (Brown, Birley and Wing, 1972; Vaughn et al., 1984).

While some family members interpret this line of research as merely another more subtle form of blaming the family for their relative's relapses, the practical applications of this research indeed correspond with many of the concerns expressed by the members of the National Alliance for the Mentally Ill. If prognoses may be influenced by the emotional temperature of the family context for some schizophrenics, then intervention with the family concerning this possibility and educating family members to the heightened sensitivities of their ill relative may result in encouraging results for both the disabled person, his or her family member, and the mental health professional. Clearly the medication regimens, supportive community-based systems of care, family respite arrangements, and appropriate counseling for all involved are concomitant needs to reduce relapses of a schizophrenic person discharged back into the family environment. The research on family members' expressed emotion could serve as a helpful backdrop for families to learn more about their ill relatives and assist them in strategies for coping, while enhancing their ill relative's functioning.

Professional Power Imbalance   The families surveyed by Hatfield (1979) overwhelmingly expressed the desire to learn more about their relative's illness, obtain current knowledge, understand their relative's symptoms and behaviors, and get specific suggestions for coping with their relative's behavior in their role as caregivers. They also expressed a great amount of frustration and anger with their interactions with mental health professionals. Many family members felt that the mental health professionals were insensitive to their needs and concerns and that they maintained an aloof and uninterested manner when dealing with family members. The self-help activities of NAMI have focused on the family members' need to participate and help mentally ill people beyond their own ill relative. They want to become active in correcting the power imbalance between the professionals and the consumers (and themselves as secondary consumers). The hierarchical arrangements in which the professional as expert defines the problem, assesses the severity of the situation, and directs the treatment interventions with little family participation is now considered inappropriate by NAMI members. NAMI has developed a nationwide committee to train and retrain mental health professionals so they will know how to include family members into collaborative models of treatment and also to train family members how to converse knowledgeably and assertively with mental health professionals. An intriguing shift in the mental health provider/consumer power equation is coming about because these new family activists are organizing to alter the mental health provider/reimbursement network. By developing lists of mental health professionals of whom NAMI members approve and then publicizing these lists to other NAMI members throughout their communities, they have begun to influence the referral network of acceptable providers (as well as compile a list of unacceptable ones). This subtle influence on the market of providers and their reimbursement mechanisms is immediately noticed by private mental health providers, the insurance companies, and the public mental health sector, which develop the purchase-of-service contracts. Pressure to include or not include a provider for reimbursement eligibility is becoming a new political strategy among the advocates for the mentally ill.

Lobbying and Political Clout   The discussions among members of self-help groups have been influential in assisting families to confront the public stigma of mental illness and openly accept and inform others that there is a mentally ill person in the family. This new willingness to speak out on behalf of a mentally ill relative has been extremely effective in educating legislators and policy makers about the needs of this underserved group. Many family members are now becoming active as members of community mental health center boards, advisory committees, state and local planning boards, and as lobbyists for improved programs and legislative reforms.

An example of the new political clout of families as advocates may be seen in new legislation passed in several states. New laws mandate that family members of even an adult mentally ill person must be notified if there is to be a psychiatric hospitalization, if the person is to be released, transferred, becomes ill, is injured, or dies, *unless* the patient expressly requests that this information not be provided to his or her family members. Other legislation that is intended to ease the involuntary commitment procedures before a person becomes dangerous to self or others has been successfully passed through the efforts of the family advocacy movement. Legislation in some states has language that utilizes only an "obviously ill" criterion to commit a person with a mental illness into a psychiatric facility involuntarily. Thus, the family advocacy movement has been quite successful in reframing the image of the relatives of mentally ill people. They are changing the public image of family members from pathogens to caregivers; from interferers to facilitators; and from adversaries to support systems (Bernheim, 1987). They also have been shifting their focus from passive to active, from personal to public, and from silent individual sufferer to vocal group lobbyists for change.

But Who Is the Consumer?

Agnes Hatfield, in her book *Families of the Mentally Ill: Meeting the Challenges* (1987), includes a chapter called "Consumer Issues in Mental Illness." She suggests that consumer empowerment has raised the issues of consumer-provider relationships, definitions of mental illness, cost effectiveness in treatment, professional training, and ways of financing care (1987:35). She notes that only a few years ago, a family in crisis due to the onset of a family member's mental illness had few places to turn for effective help. She contends that the National Alliance for the Mentally Ill came into being with "effective consumerism" as a primary goal. NAMI has documented the paternalistic style of most mental health professionals that either bred passive, compliant consumers or consumers that dropped out of treatment. In either case, the consumer's voice was of little concern to the mental health professionals. "Good patients" were cooperative, compliant, agreeable, and uncritical of the professional's interventions. Families also were expected to behave in a similarly uncritical and passive manner. Providers rarely were concerned by consumers' evaluations and particularly in the area of mental illness, a consumer's judgment was often by definition suspect, further protecting the professional's authority.

Hatfield, interestingly, never distinguishes between the needs of the client/consumer and those of the relative. Her writings discuss strategies of advocacy as if the primary consumer (the person with the psychiatric disability) were identical with his or her family members. In some instances this is true. However, in many cases, it is not.

Voices of Conflict

The advocacy movement for the seriously mentally ill has grown dramatically in the last decade. The largest growth has occurred in the movement organized by relatives of mentally ill individuals. However, the primary consumers—the mentally ill people themselves— are also attempting to organize and have developed several advocacy/self-help activities across the nation. While the convergence of these two advocacy groups augurs well for improved services, increased funding, increased public awareness, and decreased stigma about mental illness, there are also definite differences within the perspectives of the family members and the ill person. These differences have often been highlighted during legislative debates used by governments to delay or avoid supporting particular legislation and legislative initiatives. A time-honored belief about successful lobbying is to insure that no similarly aligned interest group or relevant party enters the legislative hearing room with an opposing (or even slightly different) approach to a proposed funding bill or piece of legislation. If, for example, the local NAMI chapter is attempting to modify existing commitment legislation, but the local Mental Health Association chapter opposes it along with support from the patient's self-help groups, the ACLU, and the local Office of Protection and Advocacy, the best guess is that no change will occur. Until the "self-interested" groups can form a united position, it is unlikely the politicians will choose from among the different positions and select one to support. The profession of politics is one of compromise and politicians prefer to follow the lead of a united group rather than pick among competing interests—particularly when the interests include mentally ill persons, their families, legal advocates, and mental health professionals. Thus, whereas a decade ago no one articulately spoke for the interests of the mentally ill, now there are several different voices expressing somewhat different concerns that at times are hard to reconcile.

Consumer Orientations: The Ex-patients' and Consumers' Needs

Along with the development of the National Alliance for the Mentally Ill came a marked increase in the advocacy efforts concerning the delivery of mental health services organized by consumers and ex-patients. In recognition of this national effort, the National Institute of Mental Health began sponsoring conferences specifically for ex-patients and consumers to provide them an opportunity to meet with one another as well as express their concerns about the existing service delivery system (and have these concerns heard). Nationally there are two streams of consumer groups. They are the National Alliance of Mental Patients (NAMP) that grew out of the liberation movement and the National Mental Health Consumers' Association (NMHCA), begun in 1985 and organizing since among the consumer conferences and the current clients of the community-based mental health programs. Both groups want to protect patients' rights and work for alternative mental health approaches and system-wide changes. They differ in their stance toward the existing mental health system, with NAMP taking a more confrontational position and NMHCA being more conciliatory. Both groups have joined in alliances on such specific issues as getting more ex-patient participation in the new federally mandated protection and advocacy system. The main issue on which the groups take a different position is that of forced treat-ment, which NAMP opposes unequivocally and on which NMHCA takes no position.

The National Mental Health Consumers' Association states its pur-poses as being for consumers' "rights, responsibility, and respect" (*Your Choice*, 1987). It has adopted a NMHCA Constitution with a Bill of Rights and the following goals:

1. To protect and advocate for the rights of mental health con-sumers.
2. To further the development of local, user-controlled alterna-tives, linked by a national clearinghouse.
3. To improve the quality of life for mental health consumers by ending discrimination in housing and employment, address-ing the needs of homeless people and poor people, and ad-vocating for increased public benefits.
4. To ensure the mental health system's responsiveness and ac-countability to mental health consumers by gaining consumer representation on mental health decision making bodies.
5. To educate and influence the media concerning the importance of a positive portrayal of mental health consumers and sen-sitivity to our issues and concerns, thereby fighting stigma in the community.

The Mental Health Liberation Movement   Judi Chamberlin has been an outspoken mental health consumer activist for over a decade.

Her "branch" of the consumer/self-help movement, now called the National Alliance of Mental Patients, clearly states that they feel that they have been "hurt and dehumanized by a system that claimed to help" and that "[most consumers] found true help when we reached out to one another" (Chamberlin, 1987). She contends that certain beliefs are basic to the mental patients' liberation movement. Her group has the following credo:

1. We are individuals, not labels or diagnoses.
2. We oppose all forms of forced treatment, including inpatient and outpatient commitment, forced drugging, compulsory "aftercare," and all other means of coercive involvement in the mental health system.
3. We believe in the necessity for voluntary, user-controlled, non-medical alternatives, recognizing that emotional pain is real and that many people are unwilling to return to a system they have found unhelpful in the past.

Recently, the two groups have gone public over their differences and each group now has its own newspaper. And while the purpose of both groups is to increase the self-help movement of mental health consumers, it is not clear how their disagreements will affect the growth of the consumer movement.

A Consumers' White Paper

In the summer of 1986, a meeting of ex-patients and consumers was held in Burlington, Vermont, sponsored by a grant from the National Institute of Mental Health, to develop a position paper on the role of consumers in human resource development. A white paper was developed: "The Role of Ex-patients and Consumers in Human Resource Development for the 1990s." It is an excellent statement of the needs and concerns of consumers of mental health services. The similarities and overlapping perspectives of the consumer group with the family advocacy movement (and later the civil libertarian perspectives) will be discussed below.

The consumers at the Vermont Conference conceptualized their concerns through four major themes: professionalism, the medical model, power and control, and economics (Blanch and Wilson, 1987:2). These themes parallel family advocacate's concerns discussed earlier, but one can also see differences with the National Mental Health Consumers' Association.

Professionalism   The mental health professional has become a target of criticism from both mental health consumers and their families. The dependence on the professional's expertise is being challenged by both groups. Family members and consumers alike are turning away from the "experts" and toward each other for assistance. Many feel that their personal experiences are valid and of more practical use to others in similar circumstances than the approaches used by professionals who have learned their skills and intervention strategies from books in graduate school training programs. Ex-patients and consumers note also that most mental health training programs do not focus on the needs of those labeled "chronically mentally ill." Rather, most graduate programs and mental health professionals still train for the "YAVIS client"—the young, attractive, verbal, intelligent, and sexy type of person that many psychotherapists seem to prefer to treat even though other clients may be in much greater need. Training models and psychotherapeutic methods used effectively for some sectors of mentally handicapped people do not adapt well for interventions with the seriously disabled mentally handicapped. Often professionals are themselves confused as to what to do and rely and focus primarily on drug therapy to control overt symptomatology. Consumers contend that most mental health professionals underestimate the real emotional stresses that consumers suffer and that they lack an understanding for their need for ancillary services such as adequate housing and community-based social support systems.

Many consumers are now loudly complaining about their experiences with the revolving door syndrome (brief but frequent episodes of involuntary hospitalizations) and/or the "prolixin van" syndrome (antipsychotic medication dosage in a one-shot syringe that lasts for two weeks). Ex-patients explain that these experiences result in a sense of low self-worth and powerlessness over their own lives. Family members also complain about the form and structure of existing mental health services that are not targeted on the seriously mentally ill and are not of much practical help. Both ex-patients and family members agree that mental health professionals who have been trained to maintain a professional distance, to remain "objective," to see themselves as the expert helper and thus the client as a dependent "helpee," represent a traditional model of psychiatric dominance that must be rejected in light of today's circumstances.

The Medical Model Dominance   Ex-patients, consumers, and family members mostly agree that the current mental health service delivery system is dominated by the assumption that mental illnesses should be treated like any other medical problem. The "disease" is something that must be controlled, cured, or changed by trained professionals. Consumers want their mental disability to be seen as a disability, with the focus being on each person's unique set of strengths and weaknesses and their abilities to cope. Ex-patients feel that professionals see their disability as a problem to be fixed and controlled and thus view the ill person as the problem rather than as a person capable of change, needing respect and dignity, and having the right to make choices and participate in his or her own recovery. The prescription of antipsychotic medications, which clearly mask and control overt symptomatology, does not cure. Consumers almost uniformly describe the side effects of these medications as unpleasant and many feel that the drugs dull the emotions that they need to experience in order to learn how to deal with them in their daily lives (Blanch and Wilson, 1987:3).

Power and Control   Issues of power and control permeate the lives of mentally ill people. Laws have been passed in every state to protect a mentally ill person from being held responsible for actions (e.g., misdemeanors or felonies) when they were of diminished mental capacity and are not capable of distinguishing the difference between right and wrong. But psychiatric patients, whether voluntary or involuntary, have generally been considered both by statute and by clinical practice to be globally incompetent by virtue of their hospitalizations and/or diagnosis of mental illness. The issue of diminished capacity is a crucial one for consumers who contend that mental health professionals (and sometimes even their family members) take control of their lives and prevent them from remaining active in the decisions that affect their lives. But the protections against convicting a person who is mentally ill have resulted in the development of legislation of presumably failsafe procedures whereby a person may be adjudicated as "not guilty by reason of insanity" or "guilty but mentally ill." These procedures were meant to protect a mentally ill person, but they also have led to an assumption in society that most mentally ill persons are not capable of making decisions in their own best interests. Thus it has been left to mental health professionals, family members, neighbors, and legislators to make decisions that at times are in opposition to what a mentally ill person wants and would have chosen.

Many consumers have experienced the situation in which if they do express opposition to a professional's diagnosis or treatment plan, their behavior is interpreted as hostile and sometimes even as the basis for the initiation of involuntary treatment procedures. People diagnosed as mentally ill often find themselves in situations in which others have ultimate control over their lives; others presume to know what they are thinking and feeling and what is best for them. Students training in mental health facilities are often initially shocked at the way professionals talk about mentally ill people in their presence, but in a manner which presumes the patients can not understand. (Unfortunately, most students ultimately model the behavior of the professionals they see and in turn mimic this behavior in their own practice.)

Empowering Strategies   The writers of the Vermont Consumers' Consortium (1987) noted that the theory of crisis intervention, used successfully with rape victims, victims of natural disasters, and acute-stage mourners, emphasizes the need to counteract the victims' feelings of powerlessness and loss of control. Clients are helped to take control over the decisions in their lives as soon as possible in order to retake the sense of loss of control felt because of their trauma (Burgess and Holmstrom, 1974). But most mental health treatments, even voluntary ones, assume that the client can not take charge of the treatment decisions that will affect him or her. Most mental health professionals do not seek client feedback or measures of client satisfaction as a reference point for their work; rather they seek acceptance from their peers—other mental health professionals with much the same point of view (see Rose, 1985, for an exception).

Most ex-patient and consumer groups are now advocating for decent housing, meaningful things to do during the day, and mutually respectful relationships with others in community settings. Involuntary hospitalizations, obligatory attendance in day treatment settings, and placements in most residential treatment settings continue the authoritarian mentality of the total institution and do little to empower and assist clients to develop a sense of capacity and hopefulness. Those who bear the burden of a diagnosis of mental illness *plus* treatments that encourage feelings of hopelessness, worthlessness, and dependency, face an extremely difficult path towards recovery. The self-help movement for ex-patients and consumers is providing more than "just" emotional support; it is providing opportunities for consumers to regain control over their lives, make independent choices, and live more independent and satisfying lives.

Economics   Being a mentally ill person usually also condemns that person to a life of poverty. Not only are the costs of care and treatments expensive, but the insurances, entitlement, and public welfare allocations are inadequate in both quantity and quality. Even those who have resources when they become sick (or who have relatives that do) can rarely protect their economic resources against the costs of the illness. When a person gets hospitalized, they often lose their job and may be forced to give up their home or apartment. Once a person is diagnosed with a mental illness, it is much more difficult for him or her to secure or keep employment due to the stigma and misconceptions about mental illness.

Public Assistance   Public benefits have improved somewhat for the mentally disabled, but restrictions and complex eligibility requirements make it difficult for mentally ill persons to obtain and maintain sufficient and adequate benefits. Medicare is not only restricted to people over the age of sixty-five; it is extremely restrictive regarding psychiatric benefits. The major incentive structure and reimbursable dollars are for inpatient care. Medicaid, which provides medical benefits to certain low-income families, has been expanded to cover some community-based services (like case management) as a option offered to the states for mentally ill persons who would previously have needed institutional care. But the vast majority of Medicaid expenses still is for inpatient care. Ironically, Medicaid *excludes* reimbursements to individuals between the ages of twenty-two and sixty-four "living in institutions for mental diseases." These are most often the states' psychiatric hospitals; thus there has been a shift in the locus of care for reimbursable services to general hospitals or nursing homes that are not primarily for the mentally ill.

Social Security Disability Insurance provides cash assistance for living expenses and could have been an important help in maintaining seriously mentally ill persons in the community. However, these benefits are based on a previously established record of employment and payments into the system. For many young mentally ill, no such record has ever been achieved. For older ill people, their previous employment record may be inconsistent and thus make them ineligible for SSDI benefits.

The Supplemental Security Insurance program is not based on considerations of previous employment, but recipients must meet income test eligibility on a monthly basis. Mentally ill persons have a particularly difficult time in obtaining the benefits due to them in the first place. If they are bounced off the SSI rolls, they are not easily able to participate in any appeal hearings to reestablish eligibility.

The Veterans Administration provides extensive inpatient and outpatient coverage for persons who have been honorably discharged from military duty. But clearly, none of these programs provide sufficient protections against the costs of a severe mental illness.

Most program costs are exhorbitant; either the client alone spends his or her resources until he or she becomes impoverished enough to be eligible for a public welfare allocation; or the family pays until it cannot do so any longer; or the person is put into a program covered by an insurance program regardless of its appropriateness; or the person becomes a street person, making do among the homeless. The ex-patients and consumers themselves note the tremendous disparities between the financial success of mental health practitioners, planners, and professionals and the abject poverty among those they plan for (Blanch and Wilson, 1987:5).

Consumer Orientations: Volunteer and Paid Advocates

Another advocacy organization made up primarily of volunteers is the Mental Health Association. The National Mental Health Association (NMHA) is a nonprofit corporation established in 1950 out of a merger of the National Committee for Mental Hygiene, the National Mental Health Foundation, and the Psychiatric Foundation (a branch of the American Psychiatric Association that raised funds for mental health projects). Its purpose is to develop a coordinated voluntary citizens movement to work for the improved methods and services in research, prevention, detection, diagnosis, and treatment of mental illness and handicaps; and for the promotion of mental health (NMHA Bylaws, 1987). The national organization describes its mission through five action goals:

1. Advocacy for Social Change: The NMHA maintains its capacity for informed independent action through broadbased volunteer participation and an identification with consumer interests. At the national level, NMHA works to enact legislation and policy and secure funds to refine the programs and services which are inadequately meeting the needs of mentally ill persons. At the state and local levels, NMHA's 600 affiliates serve their communities by organizing self-help and support groups; assisting individuals in obtaining desired services and protecting their rights; monitoring and evaluating mental health services; educating and lobbying elected officials about the needs of people with mental illnesses; and sponsoring public educational forums on mental health issues.
2. Anti-Stigma Campaign: NMHA sees the alleviation of stigma and public misconception about mental illnesses and the people who have them as an overriding and continuous emphasis of the organization. In 1960, May was first observed as Mental Health Month. Affiliates across the nation now use this activity for increased public awareness of the goals and activities of the nation's mental health programs and services. The focus of Mental Health Month is on prevention, the promotion of mental health, and informing the public about the progress that has been made in treatment, services, and treatment.
3. Research Activities: Support of research on the causes, prevention, and treatment of mental illnesses and the maintenance of mental health is a longstanding priority of NMHA. Affiliates sponsor

research symposia to inform the public of new discoveries in the cause, course, and treatment of mental disorders and the prevention of mental disorders; and to inform practitioners about new clinical applications and innovative service delivery strategies. Activities include efforts to promote increased funding for mental health research through action and advocacy. In 1985, NMHA became a partner organization in the National Alliance for Research on Schizophrenia and Depression, a foundation formed for the purpose of raising funds from the private sector to support research on mental illness.

4. Leadership in Prevention: Prevention of mental illnesses has been one of the major goals of NMHA since its founding. A major step in assessing the current status of the prevention field and determining needs was achieved with the report of the NMHA's National Commission on the Prevention of Mental-Emotional Disabilities. NMHA launched the Office of Prevention in 1987; it is designed to implement the recommendations of the report. A major focus will be on mental health promotion within schools.

5. Public Information: The provision of referral and educational information to the public is a critical service of NMHA.

The Mental Health Association sees itself as the logical outgrowth of Clifford Beers' central intent back in 1908 when he founded the Connecticut Committee on Mental Hygiene. Rather than organizing to carry out specific services or deliver services, Beers set out to create a "movement" and a "cause"—a movement that was intended to have influence and to bring about reform. Dedication to cause change, to create public concern and sympathy, and to influence decision makers is the underlying principle of NMHA's purpose (Preston Garrison, executive director, NMHA speech, 1987).

RECONCILING INTERESTS

In 1988, faced with severe cuts in the budgets in the three institutes of the Alcohol, Drug Abuse and Mental Health Administration (ADAMHA), the National Institute of Mental Health, the National Institute on Drug Abuse, and the National Institute on Alcohol Abuse formed a coalition to examine similar concerns. They met as a group and signed a statement recommending increased appropriations for research into mental illness and addictive disorders. And while this recommendation may seem trivial, since few advocates would be against increased federal funding, the fact that fifty organizations met, agreed, and signed a statement of support brought about a new phase of coalition advocacy in Washington on behalf of people with mental illnesses and substance abuse problems. (See Table 1 for a list of these organizations.) These groups agreed to meet and negotiate with each other for the purposes of establishing a single legislative agenda. The task was to find the needs and interests behind each group's own individual approach rather than the positions which were at times in opposition to one another. As of this writing, their ultimate effectiveness is not yet determined.

Table 1 Fiscal Year 1988 Coalition Appropriations Recommendations for ADAMHA

Alcohol and Drug Problems Association of America
American Academy of Child and Adolescent Psychiatry
American Association for Counseling and Development
American Association for Marriage and Family Therapy
American Association for Partial Hospitalization
American Association of Chairmen of Departments of Psychiatry
American Association of Psychiatrists in Alcohol and Addictions
American Association of Directors of Psychiatric Residency Training
American College of Neuropsychopharmacology
American Council for Drug Education
American Hospital Association
American Mental Health Counselors Association
American Mental Health Fund
American Nurses Association
American Psychiatric Association
American Psychological Association
American Rehabilitation Counseling Association
Americans for Substance Abuse Prevention and Treatment
Association for Counselor Education and Supervision
Association of Labor-Management Administrators and Consultants on Alcoholism
Association for Specialists in Group Work
Association of Adult Development and Aging
Association of Mental Health Administrators
Association of Minority Health Professions Schools
Association of Psychiatric Outpatient Centers of America
Care Institute
Committee on Problems of Drug Dependence
Consortium of Social Science Associations
Corporation for the Advancement of Psychiatry
Council of Graduate Departments of Psychology
Council of University Directors of Clinical Psychology
Families in Action-National Drug Information Center
International Association of Psychosocial Rehabilitation Services
Legal Action Center
Mental Health Law Project
National Alliance for the Mentally Ill
National Association for Alcoholism Treatment Programs   *(continues)*

Table 1 Fiscal Year 1988 Coalition Appropriations Recommendations for ADAMHA *(continued)*

National Association of Private Psychiatric Hospitals
National Association of Protection and Advocacy Systems, Inc.
National Association of Social Workers
National Association of State Alcohol and Drug Abuse Directors
National Association of State Mental Health Program Directors
National Council of Community Mental Health Centers
National Council of Schools of Professional Psychology
National Federation of Societies for Clinical Social Work
National Mental Health Association
National Mental Health Consumers Association
Phobia Society of America
Research Society on Alcoholism
Therapeutic Committee of America

10

The Joyce Brown Story

A NEW INITIATIVE FOR HOMELESS MENTALLY ILL PEOPLE

In 1987, in a highly publicized event, New York City Mayor Edward Koch "boldly" announced a new initiative to shelter homeless mentally ill people living in the streets of the city. He reopened a twenty-eight bed psychiatric unit at Bellevue Hospital specifically redesigned for these people. His stated goals were to take mentally ill people off of the streets and provide them with needed psychiatric treatment. He made it very clear that this program was not established to pay the rent for every homeless person in New York City. However, with the growing public concern about the homeless, one would have presumed that these actions would have been widely supported and seen as a necessary step to prevent the continuing neglect of homeless people with mental illnesses. Yet Mayor Koch found himself in the middle of a huge controversy, complete with national press coverage and criticism from almost every mental health advocacy group. He seemed genuinely surprised at the reaction and outcry against his new policy.

The reactions and harsh criticisms closely parallel the arguments of the mental health advocates described in the previous chapters. The "battle lines" were sharply drawn between attorneys advocating for their clients and mental health professionals advocating for theirs.

THE CASE OF AN ALLEGEDLY MENTALLY ILL PATIENT AGAINST THE NEW YORK CITY HEALTH AND HOSPITALS CORPORATION AND BELLEVUE HOSPITAL

In early October 1987, Mayor Koch announced that he had sent out city mental health workers to "round up" seriously mentally ill homeless people living on the streets. If their self-neglect was deemed to be so severe that they presented a danger of bringing harm to themselves, they would be transported to Bellevue Hosptial pursuant to Section

9.39 of the New York State Mental Hygiene Law. This law provides that a person may be involuntarily hospitalized by an admitting psychiatrist for a period of fifteen days and authorizes a hospital to receive and retain as a patient "any person alleged to have a mental illness for which immediate observation, care, and treatment in a hospital is appropriate and which is likely to result in serious harm to himself or others." Likelihood to result in serious harm means:

1. Substantial risk of physical harm to himself as manifested by threats of or attempts at suicide or serious bodily harm or other conduct demonstrating that he is dangerous to himself, or

2. A substantial risk of physical harm to other persons as manifested by homicidal or other violent behavior by which others are placed in reasonable fear of serious harm.

Persons requiring continuing treatment may be retained (against their will) in the hospital upon the certificates of two examining physicians, accompanied by an application for admission of persons. A patient may thus be retained and treated for up to sixty days unless he or she requests a hearing on the question of involuntary retention. If no hearing is requested or no specific period of retention has been established by the court, the hospital director must seek additional judicial approval if he or she wishes to retain a patient beyond the sixty-day period. New York State laws are similar to those of most of the states attempting to protect the rights of citizens and at the same time provide for the needs of seriously mentally ill people.

The first test case of Mayor Koch's new program involved a homeless woman living near a hot air vent on New York City's Upper East Side. Most of the elements in the case of Ms. Joyce Brown versus the New York City Health and Hospitals Corporation and Bellevue Hospital are not in dispute, but the interpretations of the facts vary significantly. Ms. Brown requested that the press be permitted to follow her proceedings, so the elements of the case have already been made available to the public; thus the issue of confidentiality has not been breached here. (Ms. Brown prefers to be called Billy Boggs, a name she took as a result of her interest in a television personality. Her names will be used interchangeably depending on the material quoted.)

The case quickly became polarized, with attorneys for the city defending the mental health department's actions and attorneys from the American Civil Liberties Union defending Ms. Brown's right to live as she wished. All the attorneys agreed and stated emphatically at the beginning of Ms. Brown's commitment hearing that no one was asserting that *all* homeless persons were mentally ill or that they required involuntary hospitalization and treatment. Nor was there any attempt to argue that mentally healthy persons do not have the *right* to live on the streets if they choose to do so. Thus, the only question debated in this case was whether a woman named Ms. Joyce Brown suffered from a mental illness, was in need of hospitalization, and would be placed at substantial risk if untreated.

The Facts of the Case

A forty-year old black woman known as Billy Boggs (Ms. Joyce Brown) had been frequently visited by staff members of a city social service project to help the homeless. The agency visited Ms. Brown "at her location on 65th Street and Second Avenue." (Quoted material in this section is taken from the Appellants' Brief, Peter Zimroth Corporation Counsel, November 18, 1987.) During one such visit, the project's psychiatrist determined that Ms. Brown was "severely mentally ill and that she needed immediate observation, care, and treatment in a hospital since she presented a danger of serious harm to herself" (p. 3). Believing that Ms. Brown came under the provisions of the state's mental hygiene law, the psychiatrist arranged for her to "be transported" to the emergency room at Bellevue Hospital. She was examined by an emergency room psychiatrist who confirmed the diagnosis of mental illness and concurred that Ms. Brown needed immediate hospitalization. The next day, Ms. Brown gave notice that she wished to challenge her involuntary hospitalization and requested a hearing.

After three full days of hearings and the testimony of eleven witnesses, Acting Manhattan Supreme Court Justice Robert Lippmann found Ms. Brown to be "rational, logical, coherent," and directed that the petitioner be released from the hospital and thus free to return to her life on a hot air vent on Second Avenue. The judge noted that there was substantial disagreement among the several psychiatrists as to the extent (and even existence) of mental illness and/or her likelihood to become dangerous. He explained that "in fact, the doctors are nearly diametrically opposed in their assessment of Joyce Brown's condition and in their predictions as to whether she is likely to cause herself or others harm." After extensively interviewing Ms. Brown himself, the judge believed that she was able to "panhandle" enough money to buy a good meal and it was at best speculative as to whether she needed to be treated in a psychiatric hospital.

Judge Lippmann found that there was not clear and convincing evidence that Ms. Brown had a mental illness or that was there a substantial likelihood that she would bring harm to herself or others.

The judge commented that although Ms. Brown's lifestyle did not conform to conventional standards and might offend "aesthetic senses," she seemed to be able to function independently and care for her essential needs. He added that Ms. Brown seemed lucid, rational, well oriented, and articulate, and provided reasonable explanations for her behavior. He reported that she displayed a sense of humor, pride, a fierce independence of spirit, and quick mental reflexes. And he found that even if Joyce Brown were suffering from a mental illness, there was no clear and convincing evidence that there would be a substantial likelihood that it would result in a serious physical injury to herself or others. There was no "real and present danger" that imminent harm would befall her if she was not hospitalized.

To the point of why she refused to live in a shelter for homeless people, Judge Lippmann stated that her comments may have revealed more about conditions of shelters in New York City than about Joyce Brown's mental state. He noted that her reluctance to move into a city shelter "might prove in fact she's quite sane." He concluded his findings by saying that "though homeless, she copes, she is fit, she survives."

Thus the nub of the problem: Was Joyce Brown mentally ill and a danger to herself and others such that the city might involuntarily bring her into psychiatric treatment "for her own good"? Or was the city overstepping its bounds by committing her to a hospital and thus perpetrating a massive deprivation of liberty? Attorneys for the city mental health department immediately appealed the ruling. The next day, Justice Smith of the New York Supreme Court of Appeals granted an interim stay of the release order pending a determination by a full panel of the Appellate Court. Ms. Brown was ordered to remain at Bellevue Hospital while city officials appealed the lower court ruling.

Issues

Several issues were debated during the commitment hearing of Ms. Brown and the appeal of the finding not to commit her to Bellevue Hospital. These issues underscore the problems inherent in defining the scope of mental illness, the different professional perspectives on the problem, and the tension inherent between a person's right to liberty and his or her need for psychiatric treatment (even though unwanted).

Hostile to Help   An interesting and at times tragic irony is that the very act of refusing to accept psychiatric services offered may be defined as evidence that a mental illness exists. Perhaps this "Catch

22" is unique among mental health experts, since their authoritative expertise prevents the allegedly ill person from successfully challenging the professional's diagnosis. By seeing the act of refusing help from a psychiatrist as "hostile," a hierarchical structure is established that makes it almost impossible for the alleged mentally ill person to explain his or her circumstances. Only by accepting the psychiatrist's assessment that one is mentally ill, may an allegedly mentally ill person be seen as not mentally ill!

In the case of Joyce Brown, this was clearly stated by a social worker in the city's project for the homeless who told the judge at the commitment hearing that Ms. Brown should be in the hospital because she refused to accept the services she requires. The social worker added that Ms. Brown regularly chased the project people away, consistently refusing a host of services, and shouted at them to "leave me the fuck alone." She testified that she had seen Ms. Brown's behavior deteriorate and she was becoming more hostile and aggressive over time. This social worker, as well as the other project staff people, eloquently described their concern for Ms. Brown's well-being. They explained that she was not adequately clothed for the cold weather, was barefoot, smelled of urine, and was generally dirty and disheveled. The Project staff members were concerned that Ms. Brown was not eating properly and was endangering herself through her risky behaviors and bizarre lifestyle on the streets. It seemed patently clear to the staff that these behaviors were inappropriate and that it was necessary to intervene whether the client concurred or not.

To the issue of whether Ms. Brown could live successfully in the community, the social worker reported that she could not because she would not accept or access any of the services offered by the project, including food, clothing, shelter, showers, and medical or psychiatric care. To the question of whether a less restrictive alternative could be found for Ms. Brown, the social worker commented that Ms. Brown could not be an outpatient because "given her level of self-care, she will deteriorate in a few days" (p. 11, Appellant's Brief). An attorney defending Ms. Boggs described this type of social work intervention as "coercive advocacy." He commented with some irony that he saw the social worker's interventions as becoming more and more aggressive and coercive, at the very time she was accusing Ms. Brown of aggressive behavior in refusing to accept her help!

Danger to Self or Others   In an effort to convince the hearing judge that Ms. Brown was a danger to herself, several mental health experts from New York City's mental health department were brought into the hospital hearing room to report on Ms. Brown's lifestyle. Some stated that Ms. Brown's inappropriate clothing in cold weather, her poor self-care, and her angry, threatening gestures invited assaults that would likely cause her harm in the future. Her bizarre habit of folding money into the cracks of the city's sidewalks and her use of sexually explicit and crude language were described as inappropriate behaviors likely to bother other people who might then cause Ms. Brown harm. Several people testified that they had seen or heard about the fact that Ms. Brown had run in front of traffic while trying to throw some clothing back at a project staff person who was trying to help her. This behavior was seen as dangerous and potentially suicidal.

As discussed in Chapter 8, psychiatrists (like all other people) have an extremely difficult time *predicting* future dangerous behavior, yet they are asked to do so by the courts in determining the need for involuntary hospitalizations. One doctor testifying as an expert witness stated that many psychiatric patients have excellent skills in adapting and organizing themselves temporarily in settings such as emergency rooms, and may mask the signs of serious psychosis. A psychiatrist must use and evaluate the *history* of a patient (such as running in front of traffic) to determine if the past dangerous behaviors might suggest future, potentially suicidal behavior. This would indicate that a person was in need of psychiatric treatment in order to prevent a future deterioration—even though the person may look and seem mentally sound in the present.

A pattern of increasingly hostile and threatening behavior may be seen from a clinical point of view as evidence *precipitating* the need for hospitalization. One psychiatrist who examined Ms. Brown diagnosed her as "paranoid schizophrenic" and explained that she would be at great risk of harm in the future if released. He described Ms. Brown as having defects of thinking that one finds in schizophrenia. Of direct concern to Ms. Brown's petition for release, this doctor expressed the view that while some homeless people could live safely in the streets, Ms. Brown did not have the capacity to do so, due to her impairment of thought, judgment, insight, and inability to negotiate life in the street community. He concluded that if left untreated, Ms. Brown would deteriorate and that her provocative behavior and self-neglect would put her at risk.

An interesting issue here was the psychiatrists' use of the data that Ms. Brown had run in front of moving cars. This behavior was uniformly noted by the psychiatrists as evidence of dangerous behavior. Ms. Brown admitted that she had run out into the street once and thrown a pair of pants at the project worker (who was already in the street). Ms. Brown commented that she did not want the pants and that her actions should not be of concern to anyone else but herself and that she thought she had the right to cross the streets as she wished.

Has a Mental Illness   Was Joyce Brown mentally ill? In order to involuntarily commit a person to a hospital for psychiatric treatment, the person must be found to have a mental illness. Ms. Brown was examined by four psychiatrists employed by the city's mental health system and their conclusions were that she was suffering from a mental illness called schizophrenia, paranoid type. The doctors cited evidence that Ms. Brown had a thought disorder in which she would transfer her thinking from one thought to another without any logical sequence. All agreed that Ms. Brown wore dirty clothes, had an unkempt appearance, and smelled of urine and feces. These facts were used as evidence of her deteriorating ability to care for herself. One doctor described Ms. Brown as suffering from delusional thinking and ritualistic behavior because she carefully tore and folded money into squares and placed it into the cracks of the sidewalks near where she lived. Her hostility to talk to the staff of the nearby social service project was uniformly described as evidence of her deterioration and a symptom of her psychosis.

One psychiatrist described Ms. Brown's "affect as loose and inappropriate; her understanding of her illness to be nil" (p. 12, Appellant's Brief). One psychiatrist noted that Ms. Brown was bright, verbal, and oriented to time and place, but she later diagnosed her as schizophenic, paranoid type, commenting that although Ms. Brown's mental condition had recently improved, this stabilization was attributed to the structured hospital setting in which Ms. Brown was then living. This doctor further testified that Ms. Brown's previous psychiatric records from other emergency rooms were remarkably consistent with her own appraisal and were used to support the diagnosis of psychosis.

Ms. Brown's attorney raised an interesting legal issue about the appropriateness of one psychiatrist using diagnostic information gathered by another psychiatrist who had on an earlier occasion examined Ms. Brown. Information from that examination was being used to support the clinical diagnosis of schizophrenia even though the other psychiatrist did not conclude that Ms. Brown was schizophrenic at that time. How much a past diagnosis influences a current diagnosis may be an interesting legal question, since such information is "inadmissible evidence" in a criminal proceeding. It is not permissible in a court of law to introduce information about a person's previous arrest record or convictions since this may bias a jury's deliberation on the present case. In a commitment hearing, however, the fact that Ms. Brown had been seen in another emergency room for a psychiatric examination several years earlier and that a specific set of treatments were ordered was now being used by psychiatrists as collaborative evidence for their own diagnosis. For example, medication sheets from another hospital indicated that 350 mg. of Thorazine (an antipsychotic medication) were prescribed for Ms. Brown three times a day and before sleep. A psychiatrist at this hearing testified that this is a very large dose of medicine "indicative of severe psychosis" (p. 19, Appellant's Brief). She also testified that Ms. Brown previously had been put under restraints and placed in seclusion, a procedure often used to control assaultive and agitative behavior.

Nevertheless, Ms. Brown's diagnosis previously was "atypical psychosis—rule out paranoid schizophrenia." Thus one psychiatrist was using the treatment previously prescribed as evidence of collaboration on the current diagnosis. She explained the inconsistency of the diagnsosis by the fact that a person would not be diagnosed as a paranoid schizophrenic without a past history of symptoms, and the previous hospital did not have case material describing Ms. Brown's earlier behaviors. This psychiatrist concluded that the medication prescribed during the previous examination is consistent with treating a psychotic, dangerous patient, even though that was not the diagnosis of Ms. Brown on either occasion.

Another psychiatrist concurred that Ms. Brown had the signs and symptoms of schizophrenia and that she was delusional and acted on her delusions. He found evidence of pathological thinking and the thinking defects common in schizophrenia. He explained that mental illness is not a stable condition and that it is common to have flareups that require intervention and then have stretches of time when all symptomatology is gone. He expressed his concern that as the disease progressed, Ms. Brown's ability to function would deteriorate if she were left alone on the streets. A fourth psychiatrist focused on Ms. Brown's delusional, irrelevant, and unconnected answers to his questions. He concluded that the delusional responses were evidence of schizophrenia.

All of this evidence, combined with testimony from Ms. Brown's sister about verbal abuse and assaultive behavior over several years and photographs of Ms. Brown living, sleeping, and defecating on the street were used to argue that Ms. Brown was indeed mentally ill, dangerous to herself, and in need of hospitalization. However, attorneys for Ms. Brown brought in psychiatrists who rebutted almost all of the earlier testimony.

Hostile to Help   An intriguing aspect of this case, as in most judicial determinations of sanity, is that the same events could be interpreted differently from different perspectives. Ms. Brown (who was consistently called Ms. Boggs by her attorneys and the psychiatrists called in to examine her and testify on her behalf) explained her "hostility to help" as merely not wishing to be disturbed by some individuals who were clearly invading her privacy. Frequently Ms. Brown justified her behavior by saying that she would have to curse loudly in order to get the project people to leave her alone. She explained that she resented the manner in which they treated her. She admitted that she disliked the staff from the social service project and told the court that a staff person had handcuffed her, placed her in a van, and took her to a psychiatric hospital against her will. On account of that incident, she developed a dislike for the project people and thus didn't want their help.

Ms. Brown testified that she was aware that the city had shelters for the homeless, but that she did not like them. She admitted that she cursed at the project staff and would not take their advice about going to a shelter. She told the judge that she would accept an apartment from the city if it were "decent, clean, and in a good neighborhood." Ms. Brown admitted to urinating and defecating on the streets (but never on herself), because the public restrooms were too far away from where she lived, and the local restaurants refused to let people like her use their facilities. Ms. Brown said that she successfully panhandled just enough money for one meal each day, but she did not like to accept money from people ahead of time or keep money on her, because she might get robbed.

Dangerous to Self   To determine if Ms. Brown was dangerous to herself, several psychiatrists described Ms. Brown's past behavior as well as when they interviewed her at the hospital. One psychiatrist said that he had looked to see if Ms. Brown had actually hurt herself in the past or expressed any thoughts about hurting herself. He also looked for past destructive behavior such as drug abuse or self-abusive behavior. His conclusion was that Ms. Brown's statements that "it was her own business" when asked whether or not she once ran out into traffic were an expression of self-pride and not suicidal ideation. This psychiatrist admitted that he had not seen Ms. Brown on the street, but her appearance and demeanor did not seem self-destructive. He concluded that without provocation, Ms. Brown would not act in ways that would likely result in harm.

A second psychiatrist used the "successful" history of Ms. Brown's life on the streets without illness or accident as evidence that she had good survival skills and seemed to have no interest in harming herself. And while all agreed that Ms. Brown had been verbally abusive to people she did not like, some conjectured that that was certainly not unusual on the streets of New York City! There was no evidence of depression that would suggest future suicidal behavior nor was there a history of violence toward others. Ms. Brown ate regularly and while her clothing was disheveled and she was indeed dirty, this was not sufficient to require hospitalization.

It was noted by the judge that Ms. Brown had been referred to the emergency room (actually taken in handcuffs against her will) by the social service agency five different times and examined by several different emergency room psychiatrists. On each occasion Ms. Brown was released because she was not found to be mentally ill or dangerous to herself. Ms. Brown described this adversarial relationship between the social service project and herself. She stated that she merely wanted to be left alone, but admitted to becoming hostile when they kept interfering in her life. She also explained to the judge that when she used profanity, they usually went away. Her aggressive behavior was targeted at the staff of one social service agency and several psychiatrists saw it as "limited and directed" rather than "dangerous and/or provocative." The attorneys for Ms. Brown argued that living in the streets was the result of homelessness and not evidence of a pathology or a mental illness. Having tattered and dirty clothes and no place to live evidences poverty, not mental illness.

Has a Mental Illness   The case of Ms. Joyce Brown rested on whether she was mentally ill. After three days of testimony from eleven witnesses, including seven psychiatrists, a social worker, and family members, extreme differences of opinion remained. The hospital psychiatrists found her to suffer from "schizophrenia, paranoid type, and that she was delusional and suicidal, incapable of insight and incompetent to make decisions." They concluded that she was abusive, increasingly uninhibited, in the process of deteriorating, and would be unlikely to care for herself in the following three or four days. Other psychiatrists, after interviewing Ms. Boggs, used language such as "rational, logical, coherent . . . intelligent with quick mental reflexes." They contended that she was aware of the alternatives open to her and had a good fund of general knowledge. Her speech was coherent; she had a sense of humor; and she was fiercely independent. She displayed no thought disorders, had no hallucinations, tangential thinking, or suicidal ideas. Her insight and judgment were relatively good and she had existed without even a cold on the streets of New York for several years. How can these be descriptions of the same person? How could a judge (or anyone) reconcile these differences?

Refuses to Cooperate   Ms. Brown clearly refused to cooperate with the social service project attempting to help homeless, mentally ill people living on the streets. Many of the "facts" described by both the petitioner and the respondent outline a woman who from one perspective is hostile, aggressive, assaultive (to those interested in helping her), but from another perspective is fiercely independent, able to function adequately on the street with a network of friends, and has sufficient clothing and the ability to beg for enough money to get her desired meal each day. From one perspective, the woman's behavior is incomprehensible, because no sane person would make the choice to live on the streets in such filth and dangerous circumstances when alternatives are available. This behavior is "crazy" and resulted in the diagnosis of psychosis (although in the legal case, it was argued that this behavior in itself was not sufficient to result in such a diagnosis).

Her own explanations for her choices were discounted by some *because* she was diagnosed as being mentally ill. Thus, unless Ms. Brown were willing to accept the array of services being offered by the city and "understand" the nature of her illness, she would be considered mentally ill. At one point a doctor noted that Ms. Brown had the delusional belief that she was being *incarcerated unfairly* [emphasis added].

Delusions?   The issue of delusions in mental illness is an extremely complex one. A popular joke says that, "just because you're paranoid, it doesn't mean there *aren't* people out there trying to get you." While many seriously ill people suffer greatly with uncontrolled fears and are unable to distinguish a real threat from a delusion, the circumstances of Ms. Brown's street life highlight the close line drawn between permitting people to live as they wish and the need to protect them, even from themselves.

Ms. Brown was seen several times tearing up dollar bills and placing the pieces into the cracks of the sidewalk. The city psychiatrist testified at the commitment hearing that this behavior was "delusional" and it seemed to have some private ritualistic meaning to Ms. Brown. But when Ms. Brown was asked about this behavior, she commented that she doesn't like people throwing dollar bills at her and that by ripping up the money she makes it clear that she is not a prostitute and will not accept strangers' money when she is not asking for it. This example was repeated frequently throughout the trial as evidence of delusional and irrational thinking. This very same example, however, was explained differently by another psychiatrist. He reported that Ms. Brown found it insulting and degrading to have people throw paper money at her and as an act of contempt she would either throw it back or tear it up to demonstrate her own respect and dignity. She was willing to accept coins when she panhandled, because that was to be used for buying her meals. Thus, this psychiatrist concluded that Ms. Brown did not have any delusions about money and merely disliked people invading her privacy and giving her money when she wasn't asking for it. He noted that accepting one type of money over the other (coins as opposed to dollars) was in the range of normal behavior, unconventional though it might be. Ms. Brown herself testified that she panhandled about eight to ten dollars a day for food and thought it dangerous to accumulate any more. She told the judge, "You know, it's dangerous to be sleeping with money on you while you are on the streets."

The Positions

Was Ms. Brown mentally ill? Was she in need of hospitalization against her will? Should the City of New York have a policy that "rounds up" the homeless mentally ill without providing permanent housing programs that would assist the homeless? Is it a violation of one's rights to be prohibited from living on the streets and begging for food? Who is responsible for caring for our citizens who behave differently and want to live their lives differently? Are we responsible to care for them? Provide programs for them? Force them into care? Or do they have the "right" to remain homeless and even "die with their rights on"?

The problems of the seriously and persistently mentally ill are extremely complex. Because there is so little agreement in this field as to even the cause of the problem, it is extremely difficult to organize the mental health professionals, mental health attorneys, advocates, family members, and the mentally ill people themselves into a unified force that will agree to devise programs, support policies, change laws, and find strategies to end this neglect.

HOW TO PROTECT AND DEFEND?

Clearly, functional and judgmental impairment can bring people into situations which decrease their well-being and safety. Whether this is due to a mental illness, substance abuse, or some other disability, these people at times need to be both protected from their situation and defended from losing their cherished freedoms. Many impaired individuals who face endangering situations fail to recognize the danger, do not know how to obtain help that is available, do not want the help that is offered, or mistrust and/or misunderstand potential helpers. For these reasons, many such people are not brought into the system (or to anyone's attention) until the situation has become an emergency or a life-threatening situation.

In an earlier era, individuals who behaved in a bizarre manner or evidenced an inability to care for themselves would likely be institutionalized where at least the basics of food, clothing, and shelter would be provided. But as the standards for involuntary commitment have been substantially raised (and properly so), the needed community alternatives and monitoring functions to support those with impaired judgments have not emerged. It is now widely agreed that the mental health system has failed to fill the protective functions that were once served by insane asylums. Today, hoards of disorganized, noncompliant, mentally ill persons are just being ignored, neglected, and even abused.

In almost every community in America, the responsibility for the seriously mentally ill has been returned to family members or the criminal justice system. Voluntary mental health services for those who have insurance coverage and choose to participate in the array of services offered usually receive adequate help. However, for the millions of persistently and seriously mentally ill persons who do not want to take antipsychotic medications (that manage *them* as well as their symptoms and frequently have known debilitating side effects), or do not want to participate in the psychiatrically dominated mental health programs in the community, the present alternative is no service at all.

The responsibility for these people has been given over to the courts and the judicial system. The common operating procedure is to wait until a person is seen actually committing a violent act or has deteriorated to a life-threatening situation. Then the judicial system can begin commitment proceedings to force a person into treatment.

This problem easily gets polarized and characterized as a debate between civil libertarians who oppose any civil commitment and mental health experts who decry the lack of laws to force people into the treatment they need. However, a middle-ground position is clearly where the solution lies. If an array of voluntary, appropriate, community-based alternatives were developed, a seriously mentally ill person would not face the dilemma of life in the streets or institutionalization in a psychiatric ward. Those who argue that the solution to the problems of mentally ill people is merely more and stiffer commitment laws that more efficiently coerce people into treatment see only a part of the puzzle. A larger conception of the problem includes the need for housing, income support, transitional employment training programs, medical care, and perhaps a lifetime of intermittent but supportive care services.

The policy of deinstitutionalization that shifted people from the hospital to the community, along with new medications and new federal insurance supports (Medicaid, SSI, SSDI), allowed seriously mentally ill people to live outside of state hospitals. But as the unintended consequences of these policies became clear, millions of people left the hospital and lost the spectrum of services to which they had become accustomed. Young, newly ill people have never lived in a hospital, never been admitted to one, nor are they receiving the comprehensive services they need in the community. Now, however, rather than noting the lack of funds and concern by the state and local governments to protect these vulnerable citizens, politicians and the public have begun "blaming the victim" for not partaking of the few types of services that the community offers. An aligned principle often asserted by mental health professionals and civil libertarians is that services should be provided only to those who want them. While acknowledging that most disturbed persons could not be expected to understand the complex bureaucratic procedures of mental health clinics nor to meet the scheduled appointments set up primarily for the convenience of the clinic's staff, this is exactly the system of care offered in the community. Many young, newly diagnosed schizophrenics who have never been hospitalized are now labeled "chronically mentally ill and resistant to treatment." But what are they resisting? Inappropriate, nonparticipatory, psychiatrically dominated mental health services with a narrow medical/disease focus?

Most endangered persons can be served through aggressive, persistent, persuasive approaches and regular monitoring. Outreach programs using noncoercive approaches have been quite successful (Cohen et al., 1984; Stein and Test, 1985). At times, however, involuntary intervention is essential to prevent serious harm.

From the late 1970s to the present, there has been a growing expression of doubt about the wisdom of relying too heavily on the dangerousness standard for civil commitment. The dangerousness standard has been seen increasingly as an unnecessary or ineffective due process measure for restricting professional discretion in an effort to ensure that people obtain needed psychiatric treatment. As a result, most states are in the process of rewriting their commitment statutes and some are trying to craft legislation enacting involuntary *outpatient* commitment procedures for chronically mentally ill people. The pendulum appears to be shifting again towards the reliance on the skills of mental health professionals as society attempts to balance the rights and liberties of individuals with the states' role to protect and care for its seriously mentally ill. Mulvey et al. (1987), in a discussion of the newer forms of "benevolent coercion" (i.e., involuntary outpatient commitments), suggest that these strategies have consistently failed to result in innovative community-based treatments. They suggest that inadequate resources follow the new attempts, so it is questionable whether new efforts really fail or whether perhaps they were never funded adequately at the outset. Secondly, many new tasks required of the same agencies are merely subsumed into their standard operating procedures so that the new efforts are never implemented. New research on implementation analysis indicates that new agencies with a single focus are necessary to bring about a new service approach. New money and even new personnel with a different set of objectives within existing agencies rarely are able to produce change successfully. Of course, new legislation that commits people to community-based services that are underfunded, inadequate, and inappropriate are certainly most likely to fail.

It seems tragic that the mental health policy for the City of New York in November 1988, as played out in the case of Ms. Joyce Brown, seems to have been polarized into two postions: commit her as an involuntary patient in a psychiatric hospital or require her to live in a shelter for homeless street people. Certainly this was not the choice expected by the supporters of the deinstitutionalization movement, mental health professionals, family members of seriously mentally ill people, or consumers of mental health services themselves.

11

Managing Solutions

THE PROBLEMS

Over the last ten chapters, the problems of people with serious mental illnesses have been delineated. As discussed, the problem definition varies significantly with the definer of the problem, be it the ill person himself (or herself), their family members, a mental health professional, a researcher, a program planner, a state hospital employee, a program administrator, an attorney, an advocate, or a legislator. Each definition has with it certain solution strategies, which themselves vary significantly on all levels, from micro to macro components. And, as funding for social welfare programs has become more competitive, with higher standards of accountability and effectiveness, data substantiating success is required to attract enough support, funds, and attention to even continue the existing programs for mentally ill persons, regardless of their known inadequacies.

Meyerson (1987:1) succinctly frames the issue as follows:

> The field of psychiatry has seen an explosive growth over the last two decades in its ability to diagnose, treat and rehabilitate the chronic and disabled mentally ill. With the advent of more precise diagnostic criteria and biological probes that allow identification of limiting organic phenomena, psychiatrists can be more exacting and specific about who they treat and with what somatic interventions they treat them. Programs of psychosocial and vocational rehabilitation have grown more precise in their identification of active and effective process variables and their ability to select patients who are likely to benefit. Psychiatrists know that the impact of appropriate residential environments and stable financial supports on outcome of community adaptation and case management has become an accepted model.
>
> *Why, then, are perhaps a majority of chronic and disabled mentally ill persons unable to become part of an effective system of care?* What prevents society and the mental health professional community

from practicing the kind of psychiatry that embodies the current state of the art and science of psychiatry as it relates to these ill and suffering people? [emphasis added]

RECURRENT THEMES AND BARRIERS AND OPPORTUNITIES FOR CHANGE

Professional Resistance

Several important themes may be identified in this problem inventory. Meyerson (1987) focuses heavily on the role of the psychiatrist as the mental health professional in charge of the treatment team. Minkoff (1987) writes of a prevailing negative attitude among psychiatrists who believe that working with these patients is unrewarding and dull and that the outcome is hopeless; furthermore, there is little prestige for working in chronic patient programs. It is ironic that the helping professions subtly (and not so subtly) encourage professional value systems that downgrade the efforts of those who treat patients who need help most.

Studies throughout the field of mental health suggest that many professionals working in the field display similar negative feelings and stigma about mentally ill people as the general public does. Studies of psychiatric nurses found that they displayed increased social distance and rejection toward the mentally ill (Schroder and Ehrlich, 1968). Pines and Maslach (1978) found that staff explained a major reason for their own burnout and job dissatisfaction to be the type of clients they were working with (i.e., schizophrenics). Mirabi et al. (1985) found that 85 percent of the respondents agreed that the chronically mentally ill are "not a preferred population to treat." Clearly this resistance is based in part on society's negative attitudes toward mental illness. The prejudices of society are mirrored by the professionals at some level, coupled with the real severity of the problem and need on the professional's part to see some effect of his or her interventions.

Understanding the Need; Focus on the Interests   A "position" often states one's stand or opinion—what one has decided. A position stated frequently by mental health experts is that (other) mental health professionals must recognize their obligation to serve first those patients with the most serious and debilitating illnesses whom the public sees as most distressed and distressing. This rather noble statement, however, does not examine the underlying interests and needs of the mental health professionals—their needs, desires, concerns, and fears. All professionals (for that matter, all workers) want and need proper skills, successful experiences, and peer support in order to remain adequately motivated and enthusiastic about their work. So what incentives are needed to improve the relationship between mental health professionals and their seriously mentally ill clients?

Minkoff (1987) suggests four recommendations to be addressed simultaneously to focus maximum energy on overcoming the resistances that mental health professionals feel when working with seriously mentally ill people. First, and most importantly, he suggests that the focus must be on training. Training new professionals with positive attitudes should be the focus of all mental health training programs. Second, a cadre of established experts who specialize in this area must be identified and formed into viable leadership positions with high visibility and recognition. Third, specific curricula must be widely disseminated and training institutes established, with official recognition and certification procedures for those who complete them. And fourth, there must be a link between the professional's own development and the work he or she is doing. Realistic goals and collaborative models seem to work best for the mental health worker when forming a relationship with people so easily stereotyped as hopeless and despairing.

These elements underlie the needs and interests of the mental health workers. Fortunately, these interests also overlap with those interests being clearly articulated by the membership of the National Alliance for the Mentally Ill.

The Family Members' Struggles

William Ryan's *Blaming the Victim* (1976) makes the point that much of social welfare ideology in America resists looking at social, structural causes for such problems as poverty, unemployment, and crime, but rather chooses to see these problems as deficits within the individual who cannot make a living wage, find employment, or stay out of trouble. Family members of seriously mentally ill people find the same problem within the ideology of the mental health system. Frequently, when they seek help in dealing with the tragedy of a seriously ill person within their family, they are met with different and contradictory explanations of what has gone wrong, yet most of the theories blame the family system for the etiology of the illness.

Family members facing the reality of a diagnosis of mental illness in the family face shock, denial, panic, grief, and confusion. Yet as they seek help with managing their family member's bizarre behavior, poor judgement, treatment resistance, lack of motivation, perhaps destructiveness, and disorganized lifestyle, they quickly find that the way they see the problem is at variance with the way professionals see it. Families and mental health professionals are indeed worlds apart in their perceptions. Family members often feel that professionals do not have the firsthand experience or the inside view of living with mental illness; they often see the professional as unsympathetic and unhelpful. Less focus on the individual's pathology and more on the practical life skills and coping strategies for those around the ill client would be a preferred approach from the perspective of the family member.

Issues of confidentiality also impinge on the helping relationship between the mental health professional and the family member. While family members have strong needs for information, mental health professionals are bound by confidentiality ethics (as well as laws) to protect their client's rights of privacy. However, these issues need not be as polarized as they are today. The needs and interests of relatives are to know that their family member is safe. Mental health professionals have not seen family members as "positive collaborators" in the treatment of their mentally ill clients and have commonly withheld information about the treatment protocols and even the whereabouts of their clients from relatives. Clearly, there are instances when these protections are necessary; however, the issues of confidentiality are to protect the client, not the mental health professional. In the state of California, the NAMI successfully lobbied for a change in mental health laws that shifted the incentives somewhat in favor of family rights. Now relatives need to be informed about a mentally ill person's hospitalization, release, change of treatment facility, etc., *unless* the client specifically asks that this information not be shared.

Understanding the Need; Focus on the Interests   While family members articulate a host of issues and concerns, including easing of involuntary commitment laws, improved community-based programs, twenty-four-hour crisis intervention services, case managers for every client, respite care arrangements, and financial relief for caretaking at home among others, surveys continue to find that family members of mentally ill persons primarily want information about mental illness, strategies for managing and coping with their ill relative, and to be included in the treatment team with the mental health professionals as helpful collaborators.

These interests are clearly compatible with many of those discussed in the previous section. Training programs that assist mental health professsionals feel more successful with their clients, and which result in more collaboration with relatives who can provide relevant and helpful information about their clients, can greatly assist both. Training programs that understand the strengths and abilities of family members and see their potential as allies in the treatment team will also be in the best interests of each group. And mental health professionals working with relatives of clients and teaching (as well as learning techniques) to improve the environment of the client and the family's ability to cope will indeed have the best opportunity to see successes. The overlapping interests of family members and mental health professionals are in the area of information sharing and cooperation. Of course the client must still remain the major player in this equation, but behind the apparent conflicts between mental health professionals and the relatives of mentally ill people are major zones of agreement which could well forge an alliance that powerfully works towards the improvement of care and service delivery.

The Primary Consumer

The issue of personal rights clearly pervades the language and concern of ex-patient groups and most mental health consumer organizations. User-controlled, nonmedical alternatives often seem at odds with the commonly prescribed treatments of most mental health professionals, as well as with relatives' wishes for secure, controlled, protected environments for their family member. At times they are. Mary Louise Sharp, patient, client, and consumer, says:

> I'll tell you what you're not doing right in the treatment of the mentally ill. You're locking us up when we're not dangerous, and throwing us out too soon when we ask for help. You're drugging us until we don't know if we're on the wall or the floor. You are forcing nourishment, life; in fact, doing everything you can to make us, like you, happy. You also submit us to another reality— the mental hospital. The worst thing about the hospitals is the mindless insults—the less-than-human treatment that the staff conveys, as if not even they are aware of their words and actions. Too many drugs, restraints, and not having anyone to talk to is destructive. Once when I felt like a refrigerator, cold, with the motor running, unable to rest or sleep, they told me it was my illness. It was the Haldol. They often don't listen, and they don't expect us to be aware of or remember how badly we were treated.

Consumers, like family members, want professionals to listen to them. Sharp says, "Our disease makes it difficult enough in life; one needs respect, caring, and honesty from one's caregivers." Consumers, like family members, want a more participatory role in the decisions that affect their lives—both at the clinical level and at the program and system level. Consumers are quite outspoken in their criticism of mental health professionals who toe the line of professional dominance, strictly adhering to the medical model, and use primarily hierarchical approaches when working with mentally ill persons.

In an article written for mental health professionals, Sharp (1987) says,

> [A psychiatrist] said I was overweight, and when I said he was overweight, he said he was the doctor and could say things like that. . . .
>
> I had a doctor who was deaf. I don't see how a psychiatrist can help if he can't hear you. . . .
>
> As a patient, I have kept everything I say and do within certain limits. . . .
>
> It helps to be accepted as one is, with an illness. . . . The only thing that keeps the patient from getting too nuts is the doctor's caring. So be sure not to leave them with that worthless feeling. . . . Mental patients derive comfort from having people understand them.
>
> Don't lie to get information and don't lie about what you are going to do. A common procedure is to give a double dose of whatever someone says they take, but many times they've run out or aren't even taking it. Please inform us of the side effects of medications when it is requested. It can get so uncomfortable, it can get worse than the illness itself. Being overmedicated is like having everything wrong; a hangover and nausea, not knowing which way is up and not having any saliva.
>
> What can I say that will be helpful? Believe in your patient as a reasonable human being. Be wonderful. Consider the glowing opportunity of allowing people to think for themselves.

Consumer-led self-help groups have been used with great success, but at times have been seen as a threat to the professional's role and viability, and thus not widely encouraged by most mental health programs. Thus, whereas issues of power and control may easily polarize mental health consumers from mental health providers, again there is a wide degree of agreement in which competing positions actually mask similar interests.

Understanding the Need; Focus on the Interests   Many of the interests expressed by mental health consumers can easily be recast into compatible interests of mental health professionals. Overlapping interests can be seen in the motivating interests of both groups. Consumers are requesting more respect and a less authoritarian approach to decision making from mental health professionals. Mental health professionals also are concerned with having so much responsibility, when in fact they often do not know what is best for a client and what intervention will be most effective. Family members, too, are asking for participation in the clinical decision making processes as well as wanting information about treatments, medications, and techniques. All three groups are seeking information, seeking more collaborative strategies for problem solving, and seeking new strategies to try to improve the quality of life for mentally ill persons.

The National Alliance for Mental Illness has a curriculum and training committee that is attempting to work with schools, training programs, and universities to influence the mental health professional's orientation and socialization. Several NAMI chapters volunteer to go into classrooms to lead groups with family members, give lectures, and run panel discussions so that students see first hand the family member's perspective. These types of activities are likely to interest the new crop of students towards work with the seriously mentally ill, but also may actually recruit more students into seeing this group as a specialty field for a future career. Again, training approaches that focus on joint problem solving, shared interests, and mutual gain among consumers, their family members, and mental health professionals seems a promising strategy.

The Mental Health/Civil Rights Attorney

Attorneys over the last decade have been playing an increasingly important role in shaping the function, size, and shape of mental health services. Some have seen the major thrust of mental health attorneys' activities as not only an effort to deinstitutionalize state mental hospitals, but also as an effort to restrict professional discretion, both in terms of treatment decisions (i.e., whether to hospitalize or not), as well as with certain specific interventions such as medications and electroconvulsive therapy. And while many rights have been won, critics suggest that attorneys may have made their careers on the backs of confused and often somewhat disinterested mentally ill people. Many long time patients "won" the right to live on the streets since they were not provided adequate community-based facilities, had no rights to shelter or treatment in the community, and were no longer able to live in the confines of the state hospital.

Hindsight has made it clear that is much easier to remove people from institutions and prevent them from being admitted or readmitted than it is to develop appropriate alternatives. The courts have been quite effective at protecting liberties, but they are not well equipped to insure the provision of human services that require funding, a matter in the hands of other branches of government. Regardless of how successful class action mental health litigation was, sufficient funding was not insured and did not come about. Attorneys frequently win cases without anyone carefully examining the implications for those affected. The point of law debated may be correct, but its implications as it is implemented (i.e., where now will the deinstitutionalized actually live with their newly acquired rights?) is not the concern of the attorney.

Tragic Irony   Perhaps the unintended consequences of the deinstitutionalization movement could not have been predicted. Certainly the current legal irony, that only those involuntarily committed to a psychiatric hospital (presumably those not seeking treatment) have a right to treatment, but those voluntarily requesting treatment do not have such a right, was not the intention of the mental health attorneys attempting to win more rights for mental ill persons. But nonetheless, that's where we stand today.

Understanding the Need; Focus on the Interests   Mental health attorneys went to battle against the abuses and neglect of involuntary psychiatric treatment and there were many abuses to be alarmed about. But now the circumstances, situation, and context have changed. Civil rights protections are pretty well established and the needs of the seriously mentally ill are now agreed upon, primarily in the areas of improved and expanded programs and services. Federally mandated offices of protection and advocacy fund state agencies to investigate incidents of abuse and neglect and provide advocacy services for mentally ill people in hospitals, nursing homes, group homes, board and care homes, halfway houses, and similar facilities. Public Law 99–319 is modeled on the protection and advocacy system previously established for individuals with developmental disabilities, severely handicapped persons receiving rehabilitative services, and for the elderly.

However, attorneys still have a crucial role in insuring no slippage in the rights won for mentally ill people, as well as assisting them, their families, and advocates in achieving the highest quality of life possible. A new thrust for mental health attorneys has been litigation in the communities over zoning restrictions, restrictive covenants, moratoriums on siting community-based facilites, etc. Now community groups are hiring attorneys to keep out group homes, residential programs, transitional living units, and boarding and care homes, with special emphasis on keeping out recovering mentally ill people. Here is an obvious place for a coalition of mental health consumer groups, family members, advocates, and attorneys to *join* forces and use several different types of strategies (including lobbying, citizen action, public hearings), as well as the courts, to bring about the true intent of the deinstitutionalization policy, which was a quality life for mentally ill people in a supportive environment. Together, this powerful alliance could succeed where other efforts have previously failed. The needs of each of these groups overlap. There is a wide zone of agreement such that mutually beneficial strategies could be developed in the areas of housing coalitions, zoning committees, and professional and lay lobbying groups, all focused on providing community-based programs for mentally ill people that respect their right to choose among several environments in which they wish to live. Professionals, family members, attorneys, and consumers all have that goal as a priority.

NEW COALITIONS

Mental health coalitions and alliances have become a new effort at problem solving across the states. Coalitions are formed when it becomes clear that a long-term set of problems that affects an area cannot be solved by individual organizations alone (Rubin and Rubin, 1986). Thus, several groups join together and set up a more formalized way of coordinating actions (in this case, political action). State after state has demonstrated the political lesson that legislators listen to consumer/provider/professional coalitions when they speak together in a single voice. Multigroup, consumer/provider coalitions in Ohio, Virginia, and Hawaii attribute their recent successes in increasing their state mental health budgets and the passage of several pieces of innovative legislation to "coalition politics."

At the federal level, ADAMHA, facing severe cuts in 1988, supported the efforts of over fifty organizations representing consumers, family members, advocate organizations, civil rights activists, professional associations, labor, and academicians. And while such group support to recommend an increase in funding may not seem too important (since few would be opposed), the very fact that so many organizations from diverse perspectives met, agreed, and signed a joint statement harbingers a new phase of coalitional advocacy in Washington on behalf of people with mental illnesses.

NEW APPROACHES TO POLICY DIALOGUES

John Talbott (1987) contends that in the area of serious mental illness, we now know what to do, but we aren't implementing what we know. Torrey (1986), after studying the fifty states, reports that services for seriously mentally ill almost everywhere across the nation are inadequate. So it seems that although we know what to do, we do not know how to do it.

The Mental Health Roundtable

Several states are trying mediation techniques in managing complex policy disputes (Ehrmann and Lesnick, 1988). Agencies are utilizing the policy dialogue approach as a way to structure and manage multi-interest groups for the purposes of policy formulation. In the state of Hawaii, a legislative resolution was passed requesting the Judiciary's Program on Alternative Dispute Resolution to convene a policy roundtable for the purposes of "making recommendations for improving mental health treatment and services for people with serious mental illnesses." Over eighteen "parties" were invited to participate, including state mental health center chiefs, hospital staff, professional associations, consumer groups, family members, advocates, the ACLU, courts and corrections personnel, and representatives from the Department of Health and Human Services. The goal is to seek consensus and make specific policy recommendations. Interim tasks include improving the definition of issues, clarifying viewpoints of different interest groups, developing clearer problem statements, identifying options and alternatives, and reaching some general agreements. With legislative oversight into this process, it is possible it may succeed.

The public policy agenda for mental health is vast and complex. New approaches towards implementation are necessary to get beyond the easily generated list of problems and complaints. Perhaps in this field particularly, people are now willing to use the skills of facilitation, conflict resolution, and problem solving processes to resolve the knotty problems that remain. Certainly the time has come.

Bibliography

Alinsky, Saul. *Rules for Radicals*. New York: Random House, 1971.

American Psychiatric Association: Guidelines for Legislation on the Psychiatric Hospitalization of Adults. *American Journal of Psychiatry* 140(1983):672–679.

Anderson, Jack. "Social Security and SSI Benefits for the Mentally Disabled." *Hospital and Community Psychiatry* 33, no. 4 (April 1982):295–298.

APA, Task Force Report 8. *Clinical Aspects of the Violent Individual*. Washington, D.C.: APA, 1974.

Ayllon, T. and N. H. Azrin. *The Token Economy. A Motiviational System for Therapy and Rehabilitation*. New York: Appleton, 1968.

Bachrach, Leonora. "Asylum and the Chronically Ill Psychiatric Patients." *American Journal of Psychiatry* 141(1984):975–978.

————. "Principles of Planning for Chronic Psychiatric Patients: A Synthesis." In *The Chronic Mental Patient: Five Years Later*, edited by John Talbott. Orlando, Fla.: Grune & Stratton, 1984.

Bandura, A. *Social Learning Theory*. Englewood Cliffs, N.J.: Prentice-Hall, 1977.

Bassuk, E. L. and S. Gerson. "Deinstitutionalization and Mental Health Services." *Scientific American* 238, no. 2 (1978):46–53.

Baxter, Ellen and Kim Hooper. "Troubled on the Streets: The Mentally Disabled Homeless Poor" in Talbott (ed.) *The Chronic Mental Patient*, pp. 49–62.

Beers, Clifford. *A Mind that Found Itself*. New York: Longmans, Green, 1908.

Berlin, Irving N., ed. *Advocacy for Child Mental Health*. New York: Brunner/Mazel, Inc., 1975.

Bernheim, Kayla F. "Family Consumerism: Coping with the Winds of Change." In Hatfield and Lefley, *Families of the Mentally Ill*, pp. 244–260.

Blanch, Andrea and Susan Wilson. "The Role of Expatients and Consumers in Human Resource Development for the 1990's." Holyoke, Mass.: Western Massachusetts Training Consortium, Inc., 1987, pp. 1–11.

Bloom, Bernard and Shirley Asher. "Patient Rights and Patient Advocacy: A Historical and Conceptual Appreciation" in Bloom and Asher (eds.), *Psychiatric Patient Rights and Patient Advocacy: Issues and Evidence*. New York: Human Sciences Press, Inc., 1982, pp. 17–56.

Brenner, M.H. *Mental Illness and the Economy*. Cambridge: Harvard University Press, 1973.

Brown, G. W., J.L.T Birley, and J.K. Wing. "Influence of Family Life on the

Course of Schizophrenic Disorders." *British Journal of Psychiatry* 121(1972):241–258.

Brown, Phil. *Mental Health Care and Social Policy*. Boston: Routledge & Kegan Paul, 1985:292–315.

———. *The Transfer of Care: Psychiatric Deinstitutionalization and its Aftermath*. Boston: Routledge & Kegan Paul, 1985.

Burgess, Ann and Lynda Holmstrom. *Rape: Victims of Crisis*. Bowie, Md.: R.J. Brady Co., 1974.

Burt, Martha and Karen Pittman. *Testing the Social Safety Net: The Impact of Changes in Support Programs During the Reagan Administration*. Washington, D.C.: The Urban Institute, 1985.

Callicutt, James and Pedro Lecca, eds. *Social Work and Mental Health*. New York: The Free Press, 1983.

Chamberlin, Judi. *On Our Own*. New York: Hawthorn, 1978.

———. "Movement Sees Growth, Change and Diversity." *Mad Lib*. Vol. 1, No. 1, Washington, D.C.: July 1987.

Cloninger, D. R. et al. "The Multifactorial Model of Disease Transmission: Sex Differences in the Familial Transmission of Sociopathy." *American Journal of Psychiatry*, 127(1975):11–22.

Cohen, N. L. et al. "The Mentally Ill Homeless: Isolation and Adaptation." *Hospital and Community Psychiatry*, 35(1984):922–924.

Committee on Ways and Means, U.S. House of Representatives. *Background Material and Data on Programs within the Jurisdiction of the Committee on Ways and Means*. 1988 Edition. Washington, D.C.: Government Printing Office, March 24, 1988.

Crystal, Stephen and Edmund Dejowski. "Substituted Judgment and Protective Intervention." In D. Mechanic (ed.) *Improving Mental Health Services: What Social Science Can Tell Us. New Directions for Mental Health Services*, No. 36. San Francisco: Jossey-Bass, 1987, pp. 83–91.

Diagnostic and Statistical Manual of Mental Health Disorders III. Washington, D.C.: American Psychiatric Association, 1980.

Digman, Barbara E. "A Survey of Family Members of the Chronically Mentally Ill in Hawaii." Unpublished MSW thesis. School of Social Work, University of Hawaii, May 1987.

Dye, Thomas R. *Understanding Public Policy*. 6th ed. Englewood Cliffs, N.J.: Prentice Hall, 1987.

Ehrmann, John and Michael Lesnich. "The Policy Dialog: Applying Mediation to the Policy-Making Process." J. H. Lane (ed.). *Mediation Quarterly* Summer 1988:93–100.

Ennis, B. and B. Emery. *The Rights of Mental Patients*. New York: Avon Books, 1978.

Ennis, B. and T. Litwack. "Psychiatry and the Presumption of Expertise: Flipping Coins in the Courtroom." *California Law Review* 62(1974):693–752.

Etzioni, Amatai and Marina Ottaway. "Revenue Sharing: The Next Domestic Disaster." *Nation* 216, no. 2 (January 29, 1973):138–142.

Falloon, I. R., ed. *Family Management of Schizophrenia: A Study of Clinical,*

Social, Family and Economic Benefits. Baltimore: Johns Hopkins University Press, 1985.

Falloon, I. R. et al. *Family Care of Schizophrenia: A Problem Solving Approach to the Treatment of Mental Illness.* New York: The Guilford Press, 1984.

Financing Mental Health Services: Perspectives for the 1980's. U.S. Department of Health and Human Services. Office of Policy Analysis and Coordination, NIMH, 1986.

Fisher, Roger and William Ury. *Getting to YES. Negotiating Agreement Without Giving In.* New York: Penguin Books, 1983.

Foley, H. A. *Community Mental Health Legislation: The Formation Process.* Lexington, Mass.: D. C. Heath, 1975.

Frazier, Shervert and Delores Parron. "The Federal Mental Health Agenda," in Leonard Duhl and Nicholas Cummings, *The Future of Mental Health Services: Coping with Crisis.* New York: Springer Publishing Co., 1987:29–45.

Freire, P. *Pedagogy of the Oppressed.* New York: Harper & Row, 1972.

Freud, S. *The Standard Edition of the Complete Psychological Works of Sigmund Freud.* London: Hogarth, 1914.

Fromme-Reichman, F. *Principles of Intensive Psychotherapy.* Chicago: Chicago University Press, 1950.

Glasscote, Raymond et al. *Old Folks Homes: A Field Study of Nursing and Board and Care Homes.* Washington: Joint Information Service of the American Psychiatric Assocation and the National Association for Mental Health, 1976.

Goffman, E. *Asylums.* New York: Doubleday, 1961.

Grob, G. N. *Mental Illness and American Society, 1875–1940.* Princeton: Princeton University Press, 1983.

Gruenberg, Ernest and Janet Archer. "Abandonment of Responsiblity for the Serious Mentally Ill." *Milbank Memorial Fund Quarterly* 57, no. 4 (1979):485–506.

Haley, Jay. *Leaving Home: The Therapy of Disturbed Young People.* New York: McGraw Hill, 1980.

Harris, Maxine and Helen Bergman. "Capitation Financing for the Chronic Mentally Ill: A Case Management Approach." *Hospital and Community Psychiatry* 39(1988):68–72.

Hastings, Margaret. "Financing Mental Health Services: Putting the Pieces Together. An Introduction and Systems Overview." In *Financing Mental Health Services: Perspectives for the 1980's.* Washington: U.S. Department of Health and Human Services, Office of Policy Analysis and Coordination, NIMH, 1986, pp. 1–52.

Hatfield, Agnes. "The Family" in Talbott, *The Chronic Patient,* pp. 307–323.

Hatfield, Agnes and Harriet Lefley, eds. *Families of the Mentally Ill: Coping and Adaptation.* New York: The Guilford Press, 1987.

Hatfield, Agnes B. "Social Support and Family Coping," in Hatfield and Lafley, pp. 191–207.

———, ed. *Families of the Mentally Ill: Meeting the Challenges. New Directions for Mental Health Services,* No. 34, Summer 1987, San Francisco: Jossey-Bass.

———. "Help-seeking Behavior in Families of Schizophrenics." *American Journal of Community Psychology* 7 (1979):563–569.

Haynes, Karen S. and James S. Mickelson. *Affecting Change: Social Workers in the Political Arena*. New York: Longman, 1986.

Hiday, V. A. "Reform Commitment Procedures: An Empirical Study in the Courtroom." *Law and Society Review* 11(1977):652–666.

Jeger, Abraham M. and Robert Slotnick, eds. *Community Mental Health and Behavioral Ecology: A Handbook of Theory, Research and Practice*. New York: Plenum Press, 1982.

Kesey, Ken. *One Flew Over the Cuckoo's Nest*. New York: Viking Press, 1962.

Kettner, Peter and Lawrence Martin. *Purchase of Service Contracting*. Beverly Hills: Sage Press, 1987.

Kety, S. S. et al. "Mental Illness in the Biological and Adoptive Families of Adopted Schizophrenics." In D. Rosenthal and Kety. *Transmission of Schizophrenia*. Oxford: Pergamon, 1968.

Kiesler, Charles. "Mental Hospitals and Alternative Care: Noninstitutionalization as Potential Public Policy." In Phil Brown, *Mental Health Care and Social Policy*. Boston: Routledge & Kegan Paul, 1985, pp. 292–315.

Kopolow, L. "Consumer Demands in Mental Health Care." *International Journal of Law and Psychiatry* 2(1979):263–270.

Kopolow, L. and H. Bloom. *Mental Health Advocacy: An Emerging Force in Consumer's Rights*. Rockville, Md.: NIMH, 1977.

Lake v. Cameron (D.C. Cir. 1966).

Leff, J. "Expressed Emotion in Families." *Directions in Psychiatry*, 6 (1986):1–7.

Leff, J. and C. Vaughn. *Expressed Emotion in Families: Its Significance for Mental Illness*. New York: The Guilford Press, 1985.

Leitenberg H., ed. *Handbook of Behavior Modification and Behavior Therapy*. Englewood Cliffs, N.J.: Prentice Hall, 1976.

Lessard v. Schmidt, 340 F. Supp 1078 (E.D. Wis., 1972).

Levine, Murray. *The History and Politics of Community Mental Health*. New York: Oxford University Press, 1981.

Lidz, T. *The Origin and Treatment of Schizophrenic Disorders*. New York: Basic Books, 1973.

Lipton, A. A. and F. S. Simon. "Psychiatric Diagnosis in a State Hospital: Manhattan State Revisited." *Hospital and Community Psychiatry* 36(1985):368–373.

Lourie, Norman. "The Many Faces of Advocacy." In Berlin (ed.), *Advocacy for Child Mental Health*, pp. 68–191.

Mad Lib: The Voice of the Ultimate Civil Rights Movement. Vol. 1, No. 1. Washington, D.C.: July 1987.

Madanes, C. *Strategic Family Therapy*. San Francisco: Jossey-Bass, 1981.

Magill, Robert S. *Community Decision Making for Social Welfare: Federalism, City Government and the Poor*. Human Science Press, 1979.

Mahoney, M. *Cognitive Behavior Modification*. Boston: Ballinger Press, 1975.

Mazade, N. and R. Glover. *Final Report Funding Sources and Expenditures for State Mental Health Agencies: Revenue Expenditure Study Results*. National

Association of State Mental Health Program Directors, Washington, D.C.: 1984.

Mechanic, D. *Mental Health and Social Policy*. Englewood Cliffs, N.J.: Prentice Hall, 1969.

————, ed. *Improving Mental Health Services: What Social Sciences Can Tell Us. New Directions for Mental Health Services*. No. 36, Winter 1987, San Francisco: Jossey-Bass.

————. "Correcting Misconceptions in Mental Health Policy: Strategies for Improved Care of the Seriously Mentally Ill." *The Milbank Quarterly* 65, no. 2(1987):203–230.

Meyerson, Arthur T., ed. "Barriers to Treating the Chronically Mentally Ill." *New Directions for Mental Health Services*. No. 33. Spring 1987. San Francisco, Jossey-Bass.

Miller, Robert D. *Involuntary Civil Commitment of the Mentally Ill in the Post-Reform Era*. Springfield, Ill.: Charles C. Thomas, Publisher, 1987.

Milner, Neal. "The Symbols and Meanings of Advocacy." *International Journal of Law and Psychiatry* 8(1986):1–17.

Minkoff, Kenneth. "Resistance of Mental Health Professionals to Working with the Chronically Mentally Ill." In Meyerson (ed.). *Barriers to Treating the Chronically Mentally Ill*, pp. 3–20.

Mirabi, K. et al. "Professional Attitudes Toward the Chronically Mentally Ill." *Hospital and Community Psychiatry* 36(1985):404–405.

Miringoff, Marc and Sandra Opdycke. *American Social Welfare Policy*. Englewood Cliffs, N.J.: Prentice Hall, 1986.

Morris, Robert. "Rethinking Welfare in the United States: The Welfare State in Transition." In Robert Friedmann, Neil Gilbert and Moshe Sherer (eds.). *Modern Welfare States. A Comparative View of Trends and Prospects*. Brighton, England: The Harvester Press Publishing Group, 1987, pp. 83–109.

Morrissey, Joseph P. et al. *Network Analysis Methods for Mental Health Service System Research: A Comparison of Two Community Support Systems*. Washington, D.C.: Supt. of Docs., U.S. Govt. Print. Off., U.S. Department of Health and Human Services, NIMH Series, BN, No. 6. 1985.

Mosher, L.R. and Burti, Lorenzo. *Community Mental Health: Principles and Practice*. New York: W. E. Norton & Company, 1988.

Mulvany, Edward, Jeffrey Gellis and Loren Roth. "The Promise and Peril of Involuntary Outpatient Commitment." *American Psychologist* 42, no. 6, (1987):571–584.

Mulvey, P. E. and C. W. Lidz. "A Critical Analysis of Dangerousness Research in a New Legal Environment." *Law and Human Behavior* 9(1985):209–219.

Muszynski, S., J. Brady and S. Sharfstein. *Coverage for Mental and Nervous Disorders: Summaries of 300 Private Sector Insurance Plans*. Washington, D.C.: American Psychiatric Press, 1983.

National Mental Health Association. *Blueprint for the Future of Mental Health Services: Report of the Future Mental Health Services Project*. Alexandria, Va.: National Mental Health Association, 1986.

NIMH. *Mental Health Advocacy: An Emerging Force in Consumers' Rights*.

DHEW Publication No. (ADM) 77–455, 1977, Introduction by Louise Kopolow and Helene Bloom.

Packard, E. P. W. *Modern Persecution of Insane Asylums Unveiled as Demonstrated by the Investigation Committee of the Legislature of Illinois.* Vol 1. *Modern Persecution of Married Women's Liabilities as Demonstrated by the Action of the Illinois Legislature.* Vol II. Hartford, Conn.: Case, Lockwood & Brainard, 1875. (New York: Arno Press, New York Times, 1973, facsimile edition.)

Parry, J. "Right to Refuse Psychotropic Medication." *Mental and Physical Disability Law Reporter* 8(1985):82–85.

Pines, A. and C. Maslach. "Characteristics of Staff Burnout in Mental Health Settings." *Hospital and Community Psychiatry* 26(1978):289–292.

Potasznik, H. and G. Nelson. "Stress and Social Support: The Burden Experienced by the Family of a Mentally Ill Person." *American Journal of Psychology,* 12, no. 5(1984):589–607.

Powell, Thomas. *Self Help Organizations and Professional Practice.* Silver Spring, Maryland: NASW, 1987.

Practice Digest, 7, no. 3 (Winter 1984).

Richmond, Mary. *Social Diagnosis.* New York: Russell Sage Foundation, 1917.

Rose, Stephen. "Deciphering Deinstitutionalization: Complexities in Policy and Program Analysis." *Milbank Memorial Fund Quarterly* 57, no. 4(1979):429–460.

Rose, Stephen and Bruce Black. *Advocacy and Empowerment: Mental Health Care in the Community.* Routledge and Kegan Paul, 1985.

Rosenhan, D.L. "On Being Sane in Inane Places." *Science* 179(1973): 250–258.

Ross, Murray. *Community Organization.* New York: Harper & Row, 1955.

Rothman, D. J. *Conscience and Convenience. The Asylum and Its Alternatives in Progressive America.* Boston: Little, Brown & Company, 1980.

———. *The Discovery of the Asylum.* Boston: Little, Brown & Company, 1971.

Rubin, Jeffrey. "Financing Care for the Seriously Mentally Ill." In David Mechanic, *Improving Mental Health Services,* pp. 107–116.

Ryan, William. *Blaming the Victim.* Rev. ed. New York: Vintage Books, 1976.

Sadoff, Robert. *Legal Issues in the Care of Psychiatric Patients: A Guide for the Mental Health Professional.* New York: Springer Publishing Co., Inc., 1982.

Scallet, Leslie. "The Realities of Mental Health Advocacy: State *ex rel* Memmel v. Mundy," NIMH, pp. 79–84.

Scheff, T. J., ed. *Labeling Madness.* Englewood Cliffs, N.J.: Prentice Hall, 1975.

———. *Being Mentally Ill.* Chicago, Ill.: Aldine, 1966.

Scott, Edward. "The Mental Health Advocacy Services: A Legal Perspective," pp. 42–54, in NIMH. *Mental Health Advocacy: An Emerging Force in Consumers' Rights.* DHEW Publication No. 77–455. (1977).

Scull, T. "The Decarceration of the Mentally Ill: A Critical View." *Politics and Society* 6 (1976):123–172.

Sharp, Mary Louise. "Out of the Streets and into the Subculture: Psychiatry's Problem from a Patient's Perspective." In Meyerson (ed.). *Barriers to Treating the Chronically Mentally Ill. New Directions for Mental Health Services,* No. 33, Spring 1987. San Francisco: Jossey-Bass, pp. 63–74.

Simpson, Tony. *Advocacy and Social Change: A Study of Welfare Rights Workers.* London: National Institute for Social Work, 1978.

Skinner, B. F. *The Behavior of Organisms: An Experimental Analysis.* New York: Appleton-Century-Crofts, 1938.

Sosin, Michael and Sharon Caulum. "Advocacy: A Conceptualization for Social Work Practice." *Social Work* 28, no. 1 (Jan.-Feb. 1983):12–18

Spector, M. and J. Kitsuse. "Social Problems: A Re-formulation." *Social Problems* 21(1973):145–159.

Srole, L., T. S. Langer, S. T. Michael, M. K. Opler, and T. A. Rennie. *Mental Health in the Metropolis: The Midtown Manhattan Study.* New York: McGraw-Hill, 1962.

Stein, L. I. and M. A. Test, eds. *Training in the Community Living Model—A Decade of Experience. New Directions for Mental Health Services.* No. 26. San Francisco: Jossey-Bass, 1985.

———. *Alternatives to Mental Hospital Treatment.* New York: Plenum Press, 1978.

Stone, Alan. "The Myth of Advocacy." *Hospital and Community Psychiatry* 30, (December 1979):819–822.

Sunley, Robert. "Family Advocacy: From Case to Cause," *Social Casework* 51 (June 1970):347–357.

———. *Advocating Today: A Human Service Practitioner's Handbook.* New York: Family Service America, 1983.

Szasz, Thomas. *Law, Liberty and Psychiatry.* New York: Macmillan, 1963.

———. *The Manufacture of Madness.* New York: Harper & Row, 1970.

———. *The Myth of Mental Illness.* Rev. ed. New York: Harper & Row, 1974.

Talbott, John. "The Perspective of John Talbott," *New Directions for Mental Health Services.* No. 37, Spring 1988. San Francisco: Jossey-Bass.

———, ed. *The Chronic Mental Patient. Five Years Later.* Orlando: Grune & Stratton, Inc., 1984.

———. *The Death of the Asylum: A Critical Study of State Hospital Management, Services and Care.* New York: Grune and Stratton, 1978.

Talbott, John and S. Sharfstein. "A Proposal for Future Funding of Chronic and Episodic Mental Illness" *Hospital and Community Psychiatry* 37, no. 11(1986):1126–1130.

Taube, A. C. and S. A. Barrett. *Mental Health, U.S. 1983.* DHHS Pub. No. (ADM) 83–1275, Rockville, Md.: NIMH.

Terrell, Paul. *The Social Impact of Revenue Sharing. Planning, Participation and the Purchase of Service.* New York: Praeger Publishers, 1976.

Tessler, R. and H. Goldman, eds. *The Chronically Mentally Ill: Assessing Community Support Programs.* Cambridge, Mass.: Ballinger, 1982.

Test, M. A. and L. Stein. "Community Treatment of the Chronic Patient: Research Overview." *Schizophrenia Bulletin* 4(1978):350–364.

Thomas, E. J. "Social Casework and Group Work: The Behavioral Modification Approach." In J. B. Turner (ed.) *Encyclopedia of Social Work* (17th Ed.) Washington, D.C.: NASW, 1977.

Torrey, Fuller E. *Care of the Seriously Mentally Ill: A Rating of State Programs.* Washington, D.C.: Public Citizens Health Research Group, 1986.

————. *Nowhere to Go.* New York: Harper & Row, 1988.

————. *Surviving Schizophrenia.* New York: Harper & Row, 1983.

Turner, J. E., E. B. Stone, and W. TenHoor. *The Community Support Program: A Draft Proposal.* Washington, D.C.: Mental Health Services Support Branch, NIMH, January 1977.

Ullman, L. P. and L. Krasner. *A Psychological Approach to Abnormal Behavior.* Englewood Cliffs, N.J.: Prentice-Hall, 1975.

Ury, William, Jeanne M. Brett, and Stephen Goldberg. *Getting Disputes Resolved: Designing Systems to Cut the Costs of Conflict.* San Francisco: Jossey-Bass, 1988.

Vaughn, C. E. and J. P. Leff. "The Measurement of Expressed Emotion in the Families of Psychiatric Patients." *British Journal of Clinical Psychology* 15(1976):157–165.

Vaughn, C. E. et al. "Family Factors in Schizophrenic Relapse." *Archives of General Psychiatry* 41(1984):1169–1177.

Vischi, T. R. et al. *The Alcohol, Drug Abuse and Mental Health National Data Book.* Washington, D.C.: Dept. of HEW, 1980.

Wagenfeld, Morton, Paul Lemkau, and Justice Blair, eds. *Public Mental Health: Perspectives and Prospects.* Beverly Hills: Sage Press, 1982.

Wald, Patricia and Paul Friedman. "The Politics of Mental Health Advocacy in the United States." *International Journal of Law and Psychaitry,* 1(1978):137–152.

Watkins, Ted. "Services to Individuals." In Callicutt and Lecca, *Social Work and Mental Health,* pp. 45–68.

Weil, Marie and James Karls. *Case Management in Human Service Practice.* San Francisco: Jossey-Bass Publishers, 1985.

Wilson, John et al. "Advocacy for the Mentally Disabled," pp. 3–15 in NIMH. *Advocacy: An Emerging Force in Consumers' Rights.* DHEW Publication No. 77–455 (1977).

Wynne, L. C. et al. *The Nature of Schizophrenia.* New York: John Wiley, 1978.

Name Index

Subject Index

Mental Health Systems Act of, 1980, 25;
Task Force Recommendations, 27; The
Act's Repeal, 27
mental patients liberation movement, 116
Mental Retardation Facilities and Community Mental Health Centers Construction Act of, 1963, 19
models of social action in social work, 71,
72; the actionist, 72; agent of social
change, 72; citizen social worker, 71;
milieu approaches, 15
Minimum Health Benefits for all Workers
Act, 56
model commitment statute, 125
models of psychopathology, 97–102; behavioral-ecological approach, 102; behaviorist approach, 100; humanistic
approaches, 100; medical model, 98;
psychodynamic approach, 99; sociocultural approach, 101
"moral treatment", 11

N.A.M.I. *see* National Alliance for the
Mentally Ill
N.A.S.W. *see* National Association of Social Workers
N.M.H.A. *see* National Mental Health Association
National Alliance for the Mentally Ill, 29,
36, 50, 67, 105, 118;, 132, 133, 173, 174;
advocacy, 134, 135; and consumerism,
142; consumer education, 134; curriculum and training, 177; family advocacy, 134; financial woes, 137;
political clout, 141, 142; professional
power imbalance, 140, 141; psychological relief, 139; reeducation of professionals, 133; respite needs, 136; self
help, 133
National Alliance of Mental Patients
(NAMP), 144
National Association of Mental Hygiene, 12
National Institute of Mental Health
(NIMH), 13, 16, 17
National Mental Health Act of, 1946, 13
National Mental Health Association, 132,
150–151; advocacy for social change,
150; anti-stigma campaign, 150;
prevention, 151; public information,
151; research, 150-151
National Mental Health Consumers' Association (NMHCA), 144; Bill of Rights,
144
nationally mandated health insurance, 56
negotiating the needs of mentally ill persons, 131, 132
"new biologism", 5

newly underserved, 29
Northhampton State Hospital Decree, 45,
50
"Not in my backyard" (NIMBY), 49

Omnibus Reconciliation Act of, 1981, 27,
28; the block grant approach, 28, 60;
revenue sharing, 88, 89
operational advocacy, 108, 110

Packard, Mrs. Elizabeth, 42
Packard, Law of, 1867, 42
Patient Care, 33; What works, 33, 34
patient's rights, 45; litigation, 46; Northampton State Hospital decree, 45;
"revolution", 113; unintended consequences, 46; *see* Wyatt v. Stickney, 45, 46
police power v. parental power, 127
policy advocacy, 108
policy dialogues, 179
policy models, 73–74; elite theory model,
74; group theory model, 74; incremental model, 74; institutional model, 73;
process model, 73–74; rational (efficiency) model, 74
post-deinstitutionalization era, 105
predicting dangerousness *see* dangerousness; The Joyce Brown Case, 160
President Carter's Commission on Mental Health, 25, 26
Price v. Sheppard, 46
primary consumers, 85, 175–176
private sector financing, 63; health maintenance approaches, 63
privating public social welfare, 86, 87
professional disinterest with chronic
mental illness, 172, 173
Protection and Advocacy for Mentally Ill
Individuals Act, 30, 40, 124
P.L., 99–319, 30, 124, 178
public assistance for mental illnesses,
149–150
purchase of service contracts, 92;
monitoring and evaluation criterion,
93; political implications, 93; the role of
the consumer, 93

reinstitutionalization, 49, 50
Rennie v. Klein, 47
request for proposal (rfp), 92
revenue sharing, 87–88
Right to Refuse Treatment, 46, 47;
psychiatrist's position, 48; psychotropic medications, 119; *see* Kaimowitz
v. Department of Health; *see* Rennie v.
Klein; *see* Rogers v. Okin
Right to Treatment, 45, 46; See Rouse v.

ABOUT THE AUTHOR

DR. SUSAN MEYERS CHANDLER is an Associate Professor at the School of Social Work in the University of Hawaii. She teaches in the areas of social policy, mental health, women's issues, and community organization. Dr. Chandler is currently the president of the Mental Health Association of Hawaii and serves on the Hawaii State Council on Mental Health and Substance Abuse. She has been an active advocate for improved services for people with serious and persistent mental illnesses. She has been conducting research and working in the community in this field for over ten years. In 1988, she was awarded the title of "Mental Health Social Worker of the Year" by the National Association of Social Workers' State Chapter.